Using What Works

Using What Works

Elementary School Classroom Management

Sandee Graham McClowry

ROWMAN & LITTLEFIELD
Lanham • Boulder • New York • London

Published by Rowman & Littlefield
A wholly owned subsidiary of The Rowman & Littlefield Publishing Group, Inc.
4501 Forbes Boulevard, Suite 200, Lanham, Maryland 20706
www.rowman.com

Unit A, Whitacre Mews, 26–34 Stannary Street, London SE11 4AB

British Library Cataloguing in Publication Information Available

Library of Congress Cataloging-in-Publication Data Available

ISBN: 978-1-4758-0945-9 (cloth : alk. paper)

ISBN: 978-1-4758-0946-6 (pbk. : alk. paper)

ISBN: 978-1-4758-0947-3 (Electronic)

∞™ The paper used in this publication meets the minimum requirements of American National Standard for Information Sciences—Permanence of Paper for Printed Library Materials, ANSI/ NISO Z39.48-1992.

Printed in the United States of America

This book is dedicated to

Ty and Zack,
Celeste and Charlie,
and
Emmett Gabriel

Contents

Foreword

"Don't smile until December."

"You can lighten up but you can't tighten up."

This was the kind of advice I received as a beginning teacher decades ago. I share them here and now because they reveal two important aspects of classroom management.

First, these statements reflect the anxiety that many teachers feel about the responsibility of managing children's learning and social interactions. Second, these statements reflect the sad reality that most people equate classroom management with the iron fist of authoritarianism. From this perspective, a teacher's job is to control students. Students cannot be trusted to manage themselves. Inspiring fear is an appropriate management strategy.

These are unfortunate and abiding misconceptions about classroom management. For example, just now I entered "classroom management" into a Google search. The top three results mentioned crisis prevention, incident management, and behavior challenges. These misconceptions are not confined to the general public. When I served as chair of the American Educational Research Association's Classroom Management Special Interest Group, an academic researcher declined an invitation to join our group because it "only focused on Behaviorism." Even the American Psychological Association's (APA) definition of classroom management implies that it is something that teachers do *to* rather than *with* their students. The APA's definition of classroom management reads, "the process by which teachers and schools create and maintain appropriate behavior of students in classroom settings."

Fortunately, there are people like Sandee McClowry. And books like the one you are about to read. Sandee is too modest to mention her significant accomplishments so I will. First, as the principal investigator on multiple federally funded grants, Sandee is an authority on evidence-based practice. Her classroom management program, *INSIGHTS into Children's Temperament*, is a model of rigorous research that offers teachers and schools a practical program that is grounded in the day-to-day reality of schools and psychological theories of child development.

Moreover, Sandee's work reflects who she is: a critical thinker armed with comprehensive knowledge and a compassionate heart. Her scholarship underscores that academic rigor does not—and indeed cannot—exclude care. If you haven't read her book, *Temperament-Based Elementary Classroom Management*, please do so now. It's a wonderful illustration of how differentiation applies to more than just instructional strategies. Students need teachers who can meet them where they are emotionally and socially.

The book in your hands includes summaries of high-quality research programs, checklists of effective management strategies, and definitions of policy and research vocabulary. These features make it an important addition to the libraries of schools and teachers, teacher educators, and researchers. The summaries offer a model of how to "take apart" complex designs so that their essential dimensions are revealed and understood.

Taken as a whole, the summaries educate the reader about the breadth of high-quality classroom management programs that have been tested and the range of theories of change upon which they rest. Suggestions for additional readings, links to Web-based resources and references round out this volume's contribution to the field. Faculty in schools of education will find the tips for classroom discussion thought provoking and generative strategies for engaging students in conversations that move their thinking about classroom management far beyond behaviorism.

So go ahead, read this book and then smile *before* December. You will know what works.

Joan M. T. Walker, PhD
Associate Professor, School of Education
Pace University
Pleasantville, NY
Past Chair, American Educational Research Association, Classroom Management Special Interest Group

Preface

"We need better classroom management skills!" Preservice teachers and experienced teachers are united in repeating this refrain. Fortunately, research conducted over the last few decades has yielded a number of guidelines that work. Effective classroom management practices increase teacher efficacy and satisfaction and enhance the social-emotional development and academic skills of students.

The application of scientifically derived classroom management strategies is embedded within the larger evidence-based movement in education. Changes in pedagogy are rapidly occurring! Teachers and school districts are reevaluating old strategies and replacing them with materials and interventions that have empirical support of their efficacy. Yet, few teacher preparation programs are adequately preparing educators to be informed participants in the evidence-based movement. Likewise, professional development offerings for in-service teachers and other school personnel also neglect this critical need.

I wrote this book to enable teachers, like you, to understand and implement evidence-based classroom management strategies. My hope is, of course, that the content of this book will improve your classroom management skills. In addition, I hope that this book imparts upon you a greater appreciation for why evidence-based strategies are critical for the overall social-emotional and academic development of your students.

Acknowledgments

Like the evidence-based movement in education, this book evolved despite several respites that alternated with bursts of energy. In the process, I have learned that writing books, like engaging in science, does not take a linear path. Nor is it a solitary journey. I would like to acknowledge those who were instrumental in bringing this book to press.

As the program developer of an evidence-based intervention, *INSIGHTS into Children's Temperament,* and as the principal investigator of the studies that tested its efficacy, I am indebted to the Institute of Education Sciences for funding our third randomized clinical trial (R305A080512). The successful completion of the study was due to my gifted research collaborators, Erin O'Connor, Elise Cappella, and Meghan McCormick and our dedicated project managers, Marri Davis and Dr. Jordan Morris.

I am also grateful to my recent students who provided instrumental help and encouragement at the critical end points: Parham Horn, Rachel Lacks, Andy Sickles, and especially Christina Wusinich. Finally, I'd like to thank my endlessly patient husband, Mark Spellmann, who provided laughter on days when the writing ceased to flow and tangible rewards for every completed chapter.

Introduction

Teaching and learning are optimized when teachers maintain good classroom management. Yet, many teachers-in-training and even their more experienced colleagues, find classroom management challenging. As a result, teachers are often on the lookout for strategies that will improve their classroom management skills.

This book invites elementary school teachers to step back and take a broader view of classroom management than just strategies. Instead effective classroom management requires a comprehensive approach that enhances children's social-emotional and academic development. Students, including those who are in the primary grades, are regarded as active participants in creating and maintaining a classroom environment that works for everyone.

Today's teachers do not need to use a trial and error method to achieve good classroom management. Fortunately, decades of research have identified approaches to elementary school classroom management that work.

This book presents multiple informed perspectives on classroom management in a comprehensive, yet, easily accessible manner. The most current knowledge on classroom management is presented in six chapters. Each chapter concludes with recommended readings, course assignments, and suggestions for in-depth discussions.

In chapter 1, contemporary classroom management is defined and the trends that underscore it are explored. One trend that is impacting all of the education field is the evidence-based movement. Beginning in chapter 1 and throughout the book, evidence-based teacher practices and classroom interventions are presented. The science and public policies that endorse using approaches that work are also explained.

Chapter 2 emphasizes the importance of positive relationships between teachers and their students (and vice versa!). Presented from an attachment perspective, teacher-student relationships are credited with enhancing children's social-emotional and academic development, especially for children whose early primary caregivers did not offer adequate nurturance. Temperament theory is offered as another lens for explaining why teachers have more difficulty maintaining a warm and effective relationship with some children compared to others.

In chapter 3, organization is touted as critical to good classroom management. Numerous evidence-based practices that support classroom organization are suggested. In addition, the chapter explains how the Response to Intervention model can be applied to student's behavioral needs.

Creating and maintaining a classroom community of learners is the focus of chapter 4. Enhancing children's social and emotional skills is presented as the optimal way to prevent student behavior problems from occurring. Decisive teacher actions for more serious student behavior problems are also discussed.

Chapter 5 explores the multicultural world that is reflected in many of today's classrooms. This chapter explains how culturally responsive teaching offers many opportunities for enriching children's understanding of their peers and the larger cultural world in which they live.

The book includes another broad perspective on the changing student population. Chapter 6 explains a plethora of terms used in providing services to special needs children. A variety of evidence-based strategies for supporting them are also discussed.

Although the evidence-based classroom management field will continue to evolve, a paradigm shift has already occurred among teachers. This book concludes by challenging teachers to learn more about how and why some things work, while others do not. Using what works benefits students as well as their teachers!

Chapter 1

What Is Evidence-Based Classroom Management?

If you are similar to most of your colleagues, you chose teaching as a profession because you genuinely like children and want to be a positive influence in their lives. Perhaps you had a teacher who inspired you. Many people have warm memories of teachers who contributed to their development because of what they taught or because they were remarkable role models. Some extraordinary teachers do both.

Now, it is your turn to teach. Whether you are a teacher-in-training, a veteran of many years, or anywhere in between, you are understandably concerned about helping your students reach their potential. A number of factors will influence how your students will experience their school year. Certainly cognitive ability is an important contributor to students' academic success, but it is not the only factor.

Another critical determinate is your ability to maintain a classroom environment conducive to successful learning and positive social interactions. This book is intended to prepare you to be effective in classroom management in two ways: by providing you with the most current knowledge available about the topic and by teaching you practical evidence-based strategies that you can use in your classroom.

In this chapter:

- Classroom management is defined.
- The current trends influencing classroom management are discussed.
- Background information on the evidence-based practice movement is briefly discussed, particularly as it applies to classroom management.
- The chapter ends with an explanation of how evidenced-based classroom management practices will be presented in the remaining chapters of this book.

WHAT IS CLASSROOM MANAGEMENT?

Consensus is mounting that the two interrelated and equally important goals of classroom management are:

1. Establishing and sustaining a classroom that is conducive to students' learning and
2. Enhancing students' social, emotional, and moral growth (Emmer and Sabornie, 2015).

More specifically, classroom management includes developing and maintaining positive relationships with students, creating a positive classroom community, consistently using strategies that prevent classroom behavior problems, effectively resolving student behavior problems when they occur, and enhancing students' own self-regulation.

WHY IS CLASSROOM MANAGEMENT SO IMPORTANT?

Effective classroom management is advantageous for you and your students for a number of reasons. In an examination of nearly 30 categories of influential teacher and student characteristics as well as school and district policies, good classroom management had the largest effect on student learning (Wang et al., 1993).

Students in effectively managed classrooms exhibit less disruptive behavior and are more engaged in their coursework. As a result, they achieve higher levels of academic success (Reyes et al., 2012). Teachers also benefit when they are efficacious in classroom management. They enjoy teaching more and experience less burnout (Klassen & Chiu, 2010).

WHAT CLASSROOM MANAGEMENT IS NOT

When preservice teachers envision their future classrooms, they often describe a warm, positive environment, with students independently engaged in creative learning activities. Such descriptions are underscored by a child-centered philosophy toward teaching and learning. Yet, when preservice teachers explain how they intend to manage their classrooms, they use more teacher-centered words like "control" and "order." The dissonance between these two stances can be attributed to the worries of many preservice and even veteran teachers about managing the behavior of their students (Mergler & Tangen, 2010). If rigid control strategies are implemented, the classroom environment suffers.

Effective classroom management is not about controlling student behavior. It is instead an ongoing process that facilitates learning, encourages student self-regulation, and creativity. As you will learn throughout this book, there are a variety of effective approaches to classroom management, approaches that will help you create a warm, engaging classroom for your students and thereby promote their learning and social development.

All too often, teachers' efficacy in classroom management increases over time through a trial-and-error process. Instead, by capitalizing on what is already known, you can advance your own progression from novice to expert. Otherwise, the inventive teaching strategies that you have already developed or will create during your preservice education will be replaced by rigid management procedures that compromise the classroom climate.

CURRENT TRENDS IN CLASSROOM MANAGEMENT

Knowledge about classroom management is derived from a number of disciplines including education, prevention science, child development, and psychology. Not surprisingly, the fields apply slightly different perspectives to address the topic. Despite the different perspectives, a number of trends are evident across the various approaches currently being applied to classroom management:

- *Increasingly, classroom management is based on theory.* Knowledge about classroom management practices is growing and becoming unified by theoretical frameworks (Martin et al., 2016). Using a theoretical approach to classroom management is advantageous because it helps teachers understand the behavior of their students. Theory is also useful because it can explain why some techniques are successful and others are not. When strategies fail, using a theoretical framework can prompt alternative approaches.
- *Teachers play a central role in fostering the social, emotional, and moral development of their students by fostering prosocial behavior.* One strategy teachers can employ for effective classroom management is setting up procedures that minimize disruptive classroom behavior. The goal is to establish prosocial norms so that students become active agents of classroom management. When problems do occur, effective teachers immediately take steps to prevent such behaviors from escalating to more serious levels (Emmer & Sabornie, 2015).
- *Positive teacher-students relationships are central to effective classroom management.* The interpersonal relationships teachers have with their students critically influences their adjustment and their attitude toward school (Gehlbach et al., 2012).
- *Classrooms are small communities composed of unique individuals.* Positive relationships, regardless of one's age, occur when individuals feel accepted. Being appreciated sets the stage for interactions that are mutually responsive and satisfying. Good classroom management assures all students have the opportunity to be a valued contributor to the classroom community.
- *One of the major goals of classroom management is to enhance the self-regulation of students* (Bear, 2015). Teacher strategies that impose external reward and punishment are used less frequently than in previous decades. Instead, contemporary classroom management aims to teach children self-monitoring skills that enhance their own self-regulation and emotional competence.
- *Collaboration is another trend in elementary schools.* Teachers and other school personnel share responsibilities for students' behavior and academic achievement (Murnane, 2012). Pedagogy and behavior management are consistent across the school context. To foster competent behavior at school and at home, collaboration with parents is also essential. Parents are regarded as a vital part of the school community (Sheridan et al., 2012).
- *Respect for cultural diversity is essential for successful classroom management and collaboration with parents.* In many schools, students come from a variety of cultural and ethnic backgrounds. To foster successful classroom management, teachers need to understand and appreciate the cultural, racial, ethnic, and class differences that exist among their students and their families (Gay, 2010).

Textbox 1.1   An FYI: A Historical Perspective on the Science of Education

Some members of the teaching profession view the current emphasis on evidence-based practices as a revolutionary change. An alternative perspective asserts that multiple forces with historical precedence have recently merged to evolve the field into an evidence-based profession.

In her compelling book, *An Elusive Science: The Troubling History of Education Research*, Lagemann (2000) traces the sociopolitical and historical events that have influenced the long-standing quest for a scientific foundation to underpin educational practices in the United States.

The impetus for evidence-based education came from two powerful imperatives that remain relevant today. The first is the democratic ideal that **all** children are entitled to an education that not only prepares them for life but enables them to fully realize their potential. The second is a pragmatic concern that the education of children is an expensive enterprise that would be more cost efficient if it was based on scientific findings that have identified effective education practices.

From its early beginnings, the science of education has tried to fulfill both imperatives. As early as 1890, university scholars, as well as American citizens, sought research that would identify the most effective ways to educate children. A lack of consensus regarding the best method to amass a body of scientific knowledge, however, existed among the many stakeholders such as university professors, educators, politicians, and parents.

Some stakeholders, but not all, promoted randomized clinical trials. The first published randomized experiment in education was in 1928 (Forsetlund et al., 2007). Remmers (1928) randomized students who ranked in the bottom quarter of the freshman class at Purdue University to an experimental group that received remedial services or to the control group who did not receive any additional services.

Decades later, conducting experiments continues to be controversial. In a true experimental design, participants are randomly assigned to an intervention or to a control group. Both groups, however, provide data on which the efficacy of the intervention is tested. Sometimes teachers and parents are understandably concerned that children assigned to the control group receive no intervention but are expected to provide data for the study.

The use of randomized experiments intended to grow the scientific foundation of education continues to advance slowly. Lagemann (2000) identified a number of long-standing tensions that hampered its use. Scholars in education, as well as in other fields, were skeptical that a science of education was even possible. Faculty at university schools of education used nonexperimental designs in their own research which, in turn, they taught to their doctoral students.

While researchers continue to debate how educational research should be conducted, teachers and administrators in the field want immediate answers to the urgent needs of their schools. In the last decade, however, the evidence-based practices movement in education has gained momentum that shows no evidence of slowing down.

- *More and more, classroom management is based on evidence-based practices.* Research focusing on classroom management has substantially increased over the past ten years, and the field has greatly evolved (Emmer & Sabornie, 2015). As a result, classroom management approaches have become more scientific. Classroom management strategies based on research findings are evidence based. This book will help you evaluate the evidence that supports classroom management and the practical teacher strategies derived from them.

Although an in-depth explanation of scientific methods is well beyond the scope of this book, a brief discussion regarding its relevance to education is necessary. As discussed in Textbox 1.1, science in the education field has a long history. In addition, the scientific principles that underscore classroom management are identical to those that govern the entire field of education. In fact, education shares many methodological research strategies as illustrated in the whimsical tour to Education Science City that is presented in Appendix A.

THE EVIDENCE-BASED PRACTICE MOVEMENT IN EDUCATION

An evidence-based practice movement is rippling through the education field and affecting how children are taught and evaluated in the United States. The overarching goal of the evidence-based movement is to build a scientific body of knowledge that informs decisions regarding educational practices and policy (National Research Council [NRC], 2005). Recent federal initiatives have propelled the use of evidence-based practices in education. The No Child Left Behind Act of 2001 (NCLB) defined scientifically based research as "the application of rigorous, systematic, and objective procedures to obtain reliable and valid knowledge relevant to education activities and programs" (Public Law 107–110).

In 2015, Congress passed the Every Student Succeeds Act (ESSA) (Public Law 114–195) which puts an even greater emphasis on evidence-based practices. The bill also supports the provision of multitiered services to children, encourages the use of positive behavior interventions and supports, and directs more funding toward the professional development of educators.

Today, evidence-based practices in education is an umbrella term for curricula, interventions, programs, and treatments that are supported by data demonstrating success in achieving targeted outcomes. For example, to be evidence based, a classroom management intervention must demonstrate that it enhances teacher efficacy in preventing or reducing disruptive student behavior problems.

Evidence-based practices also include mechanisms and tools for assessment and referral. As an example, an evidence-based reading curriculum might be used to identify the students who need additional supports.

Recently, multiple factors have converged to propel the evidence-based practices movement in education forward with great speed. Although the cost of educating children continues to rise, student achievement in the United States lags behind other industrial countries (Schleicher & Davidson, 2012).

Table 1.1   IES WWC Criteria to Evaluate Educational Practices

Symbol	Effect	Description
++	Positive	Strong evidence of a positive effect on outcomes.
+	Potentially positive	Evidence of a positive effect on outcomes with no overriding contrary evidence.
+-	Mixed	Evidence of inconsistent effects on outcomes.
0	No discernible	No evidence of an effect on outcomes.
-	Potentially negative	Evidence of a negative effect on outcomes with no overriding contrary evidence.
--	Negative	Strong evidence had a negative effect on outcomes.

Source: Institute of Education Sciences *What Works Clearinghouse*: http://ies.ed.gov/ncee/wwc/resources.aspx

Consensus is mounting that too many costly educational strategies are ineffective and should be replaced with those that would better fulfill the educational mission of schools (Braden & Shernoff, 2008). Moreover, the public, as well as politicians, are demanding better outcomes and more scrutiny regarding the workings of the education system. In response, most states implemented standardized testing to examine student progress by the late 1980s.

Recent mandates emanating from federal agencies show a preference for experimental designs because they produce more definitive answers than other research methods. Experiments are the gold standard used by scientists in other fields. Simply stated, experiments in classroom management compare the behavior of two comparable groups of students or classrooms that are randomly assigned to participate in an intervention or to be part of the control group that do not receive the intervention.

Federal agencies, private foundations, and professional organizations have fueled the evidence-based movement in education. The Institute of Education Sciences (IES) is a federal agency whose mission is to provide rigorous evidence for education practice and policy (http:/www.ies.ed.gov). IES created the *What Works Clearinghouse* (WWC) to provide user-friendly information for educators, policymakers, researchers, and the public to use when examining educational practices.

The criteria used by WWC to evaluate educational practices are listed on their website (http://ies.ed.gov/ncee/wwc) and are summarized in Table 1.1. Other clearinghouses also critique evidence-based practices. A number of them can be accessed through websites listed at the end of this chapter.

CHALLENGES AND OPPORTUNITIES IN THE SCIENCE OF EDUCATION

Even though the evidence-based movement is evident in the field of education, a number of challenges remain and must be acknowledged. Not everyone has jumped on the experimental bandwagon that IES has championed. Some researchers have asserted that experimental designs are not the appropriate methodology to answer many of the questions that educators encounter.

Unquestionably, schools are complex settings that make conducting experimental designs difficult. Pragmatic concerns abound when conducting randomized clinical trials in schools. For example, some schools are reluctant to participate in an experiment in which they may be randomized into the control group.

Another difficulty often occurs when evidence-based practices that were developed and tested as part of an experiment are then implemented in classrooms. Effects found in experimental design under well-controlled conditions may be lost when put into the complex daily practices of a school.

The criteria used by WWC to evaluate scientific evidence also have been criticized (Slavin & Madden, 2011). Adding even more complexity to the evaluation of evidence-based interventions is the fact that other clearinghouses use different criteria to select and evaluate the studies. As a result, differing conclusions may be offered by the various clearinghouses.

Despite the challenges, federal and state offices are using data to evaluate performance trends across large aggregates of students throughout the United States in schools, districts, states, and even other countries. Evidence-based practices also can be used to enhance the academic achievement of individual children.

A number of enlightened school districts have implemented initiatives that result in the collection and rapid interpretation of data that track the individual progress of their students (Murnane & Nelson, 2007). As a result, individual struggling students are identified early. Teachers and school support staff then use the data to develop action plans so that compensatory services can be implemented to meet the specific needs of the students.

The case study presented in Textbox 1.2 illustrates how today's teachers, in collaboration with school administrators, can use data when making decisions on student progress.

Regardless of all the complicating factors that challenge the expansion of education science, the recent mandate for federal funding of evidence-based practices has changed the field—that trend is here to stay. Both preservice and professional development programs need to prepare teachers to meet the new culture of science.

Clearly, a number of legal and regulatory mandates influence the selection and delivery of educational practices. School districts are expected to examine whether curriculum materials, interventions, and professional development programs have empirically demonstrated effectiveness before selecting them (Powers et al., 2010).

Thinking scientifically is, however, not new for teachers. Stanovich and Stanovich (2003) remind teachers that they engage in scientific thinking frequently. Teachers hypothesize that a certain teaching strategy is going to work. Then they collect data based on their observations or through testing that evaluates whether the strategy is working or not. If their original idea does not demonstrate effectiveness, they try another approach and repeat the process. This informal use of scientific thinking is highly commendable.

Other permutations of scientific thinking are likely to be part of your teaching career. Here are a few examples:

• You will apply scientific principles within your own classroom when you evaluate how students are progressing in various subjects and when you observe how their behavior influences their social and academic progress.

Textbox 1.2 A Real-World Application of Using Data for Individual Instruction—Case Study: Byron, Illinois

Byron Community Unit School District #226 is located in northern Illinois, 80 miles west of Chicago. The district has approximately 1,600 students in its pre-kindergarten through high school classrooms. The majority of the students attending the schools are Caucasian and from middle-class homes. During the last four years, however, the student population has become more diverse. The district has 136 teachers and 9 administrators.

The school district, with funds drawn from the Individuals with Disabilities Education Act (IDEA, 2004), has made a serious commitment to early intervention services for students who need additional academic and behavioral support to succeed in general education. As this case study illustrates, the teachers and district administrators work collaboratively to use evidence-based practices to evaluate the individual progress of their students.

Brady's story exemplifies how the process can work successfully to identify students who are having minor difficulties and need additional services to catch-up to their classmates. His 2nd grade teacher, Mrs. Hinshaw, was concerned about him. Although Brady had good social skills and seemed to try hard at school, he could not keep up academically with his classmates.

Brady was also easily distracted when given an assignment. His inability to sit still seemed to exacerbate the problem. Mrs. Hinshaw wondered whether Brady had Attention Deficit with Hyperactivity Disorder (ADHD). She decided to talk to Brady's parents about her concerns during their scheduled Parent/Teacher conference.

When they met, Brady's parents told Mrs. Hinshaw that they shared her concerns. They described Brady's behavior at home as inattentive and impulsive. Mrs. Hinshaw suggested that as a first step, they all should complete an evidence-based questionnaire that the school district used to assess children's behavior and then compare the results. Both parents readily agreed.

Mrs. Hinshaw completed the Conners 3 (Conners, 2008) which has 115 questions that access hyperactivity-impulsivity, executive functioning, learning problems, aggression, peer relations, family relations, anxiety, and depression. Both parents completed the Conners 3 Short Form for Parents which has 43 items. The answers on the three sets of questionnaires supported Mrs. Hinshaw's and Brady's parents' observations that Brady was having difficulties that warranted treatment for ADHD.

Brady's parents agreed to having Dr. Jonathan Stagg, the district's school psychologist, evaluate Brady at school. Dr. Stagg observed Brady during reading class using the Behavioral Observation of Students in Schools (BOSS) (Shapiro, 2004). The BOSS is an observational system conducted during reading or mathematics instruction that discriminates between children with and without ADHD. The BOSS showed that Brady was on task only 50–65% of the time compared to the other boys in the classroom who were on task 90% of the time.

After speaking with Dr. Stagg about his observations, Brady's parents spoke to their son's pediatrician who prescribed a medication to reduce Brady's ADHD symptoms. When Brady had been on the medication for a week, Dr. Stagg repeated the BOSS. This time, Brady was on task 80% of the time. His motor activities also were reduced.

Mrs. Hinshaw and the school nurse carefully monitored Brady in the classroom for possible side effects. They noted that after a few days on the medication, Brady appeared groggy in class. Brady's parents reported the information to the pediatrician who reduced the dosage of the medication.

Although Mrs. Hawshaw observed dramatic improvements in Brady's ability to attend to his assignments, she was still concerned because his reading scores were not improving. The school district immediately provided supplemental reading services for an hour per day. Within nine weeks, Brady's reading scores progressively increased until he was reading at grade level. He continued to receive supplemental services for 30 minutes per day to maintain his gains. Mrs. Hinshaw anticipates that Brady will not require any supplemental services when he is in 3rd grade.

If you visit the Byron School District, you are likely to see Dr. Stagg and the educators in PODS—which is what they call their weekly "pouring over the data" meetings. The school personnel who participate in these meetings include the principal, assistant principals, lead interventionists, school psychologists, reading specialists, and of course, teachers—who, like Mrs. Hinshaw, use evidence-based practices to help their students reach their potential.

- Student data will be evaluated by you, in collaboration with other school personnel, when making decisions regarding student progress and services.
- Parents will ask you to explain the meaning of their children's scores on standardized tests.
- Administrators at your school or district may ask your input before selecting evidence-based interventions or curriculum materials. Understanding scientific principles will help you decide which ones to recommend.
- At some point in your career, you may be asked to participate in testing whether a specific intervention or a type of curriculum works.
- Graduate programs in education often encourage their students to participate in research.

CHALLENGES AND OPPORTUNITIES IN EVIDENCE-BASED CLASSROOM MANAGEMENT PRACTICES

A great deal of progress has been made in recent years to identify evidence-based practices that can be applied to classroom management. Still teachers, particularly those who are new in the profession, consider classroom management a major concern. One of the difficulties in learning how to be effective is the lack of good role models for student teachers to observe.

In addition, student teachers often experience a dissonance between what they learn about classroom management in their university courses and what they see occurring in the schools when they are observing or student teaching. Stoughton (2007) analyzed the narratives of students-in-training as they reflected on the classroom management they observed in the public schools. The novice teachers found it difficult to integrate what they learned that placed a high value on social justice and respect for diversity with some of the teacher practices they observed. Instead, the students reported that community building and meeting the needs of individual students were sacrificed when teachers implemented rigid behavioral procedures that demanded obedience rather than problem-solving or relationship building.

The student teachers also observed that the classroom management strategies that the teachers used were consistently effective among children who were high achievers (Stoughton, 2007). The same strategies did not work among the students who often misbehaved. Those students were frequently punished and often ostracized within the classroom. Such actions only served to further fuel their misbehavior.

Like many aspects of teaching, becoming skillful in classroom management requires knowledge and experience. Learning what has already been known to work in classrooms is an important foundation for putting it to work in your own classroom.

WHAT HAPPENS NEXT IN THIS BOOK?

By the end of this book, you will be familiar with the current state of the science on classroom management because you will examine a number of evidence-based interventions. The programs differ in the theories on which they are based. Many emphasize social and emotional skills while others are focused on behavior modification or the classroom environment.

Some interventions discussed in this book are comprehensive and have multiple components. They also vary in whom they target: most are directed at students although others focus on teachers; some include teachers. The names of the interventions and where you will find their descriptions are listed in Table 1.2. Each of these interventions has shown positive outcomes in at least one randomized experiment that have been published.

Table 1.2 Alphabetical Listing of Evidence-Based Classroom Management Interventions in this Book

Name of the Program	Chapter
Caring School Community	4
Classroom Organization and Management Program	3
Family Check-Up	5
Good Behavior Game	4
INSIGHTS into Children's Temperament	2
KiVa	4
PATHS	4
Positive Action	3
Prevent-Teach-Reinforce Model	3
Responsive Classroom	2
School-wide Positive Behavior Interventions and Supports	4
Teaching Student to be Peacemakers	4
The Check, Connect, and Expect Program	3
Using a Daily Report Card	6

SUMMARY

In this chapter, the overall goal of classroom management is described as providing a classroom environment that supports students' learning and social-emotional growth. Effective classroom management is more specifically explained as having positive relationships with students, creating a positive classroom community, and using strategies that prevent or resolve disruptive classroom behavior by enhancing student self-regulation. Classroom management is essential because it not only supports student engagement and learning but also contributes to teacher satisfaction.

Rather than perceiving classroom management as controlling student behavior, current trends in the field emphasize positive approaches. Derived from a number of disciplines, contemporary classroom management includes fostering prosocial student behavior by supporting student self-regulation, positive teacher-student relationships, and respect for individual differences. Collaboration between home and school and respect for cultural diversity also are important.

The evidence-based movement, which has impacted the whole field of education, is evident in the current trends in classroom management. Scientific evidence is evaluated in the selection of practices used in schools including curricula, interventions, programs, treatments, and assessment tools. Teachers and other school personnel also use data to evaluate whether students are achieving targeted academic and behavioral outcomes.

Scientific principles are discussed throughout this book. A variety of classroom management interventions whose efficacy has been tested with randomized clinical trials are presented. In the next chapter, one of the critical components supporting classroom management, teacher-student relationships, will be examined in depth.

CLASS DISCUSSION

- Discuss the influence of evidence-based practices in other fields such as medicine or public health.
- Look up for a common over-the-counter medication on the Internet. What evidence can you find that the medication works?
- Find scientific evidence that smoking cigarettes is not healthy.
- Find an evidence-based report that explains how obesity is associated with negative health outcomes.

COURSE ASSIGNMENTS

Interview a teacher and ask how he or she learned about classroom management.

- Go to one of the following websites on evidence-based interventions and download a report on an evidence-based program. What level of evidence does the program have?

- http://ies.ed.gov/ncee/wwc
- http://nrepp.samhsa.gov/AdvancedSearch.aspx
- http://www.bestevidence.org
- http://www.evidencebasedprograms.org
- http://www.promisingpractices.net
- http://www.campbellcollaboration.org

RECOMMENDED READINGS

A user-friendly guide for teachers that describes scientific principles applied to the field of education:

Coalition for Evidence-Based Policy (December 2003). *Identifying and Implementing Educational Practices Supported by Rigorous Evidence: A User Friendly Guide*. Washington, DC: Institute of Education Sciences, U.S. Department of Education. Available online at http://www.ed.gov/rschstat/research/pubs/rigorousevid/index.html.

A practice guide for applying evidence-based practices into practice:

Epstein, M., Atkins, M., Cullinan, D., Kutash, K., & Weater, R. (2008). *Reducing Behavior Problems in the Elementary School Classroom: A Practice Guide* (NCEE #2008-012). Washington DC: National Center for Education Evaluation and Regional Assistance, Institute of Education Sciences, U.S. Department of Education. Available online at: http://ies.ed.gov/ncee/wwc/practiceguide.aspx?sid=4.

Chapter 2

Teacher-Student Relationships

The children in your classroom are members of a technologically sophisticated world that would have been unimaginable to you as a child. Most present-day children begin school with considerable technology experience. As they advance through elementary school, they become even more computer literate. Children have a natural affinity for technology.

The advantages of incorporating technology into learning are numerous. Technology learning products give children a sense of control and can help them achieve lesson goals in an engaging, active way. Moreover, if they enjoy using the e-learning product, they are likely to spend more time working on an assignment.

Excessive use of technology, however, can be detrimental to children's learning and their social-emotional development. Some technologies require only passive involvement on a student's part. Too much technology also can limit the amount and quality of teacher and student interactions. Technology can never replace the importance of responsive relationships that students can have with their teachers.

In this chapter:

- The lifelong importance of positive relationships is discussed.
- Frameworks that explore teacher-student relationships are introduced.
- Why some children are at risk for conflictual relationships is explored.
- How responsive teachers can make a difference for children with insecure attachments to their parents is discussed.
- An evidence-based intervention, the *Responsive Classroom,* which enhances teacher-student relationships is presented.
- Changes in teacher-student relationships over time are discussed.
- Other implications of positive student-teacher relationships are explored.
- Temperament theory is offered as an alternative perspective on viewing teacher-student relationships.
- A temperament-based intervention, *INSIGHTS into Children's Temperament,* is introduced.
- Teacher actions that develop and improve teacher-student relationships are suggested.

THE IMPORTANCE OF POSITIVE RELATIONSHIPS

Relationships have a profound effect on individuals throughout their lifespan. When relationships are positive, they provide joy and a sense of worth, acceptance, and validation (Reis et al., 2000).

Close relationships elicit strong emotions because they are particularly important to the individuals involved. The feelings that underscore such relationships are replete with expectations on how the people involved in the relationships should interact with each other. One's identity is affected by the feedback received in the course of these interactions.

Over time and based on the many moment-to-moment interactions that occur in their classrooms, teachers develop relationships with their students. The tenor of those relationships differ based on how a teacher interacts with each student and with the classroom as a whole. Teaching and learning are optimized when teachers and their students have positive relationships.

FRAMEWORKS FOR EXPLORING TEACHER-STUDENT RELATIONSHIPS

Several frameworks are used to explore the impact of teacher-student relationships on children's social-emotional and academic development. From an ecological perspective (Bronfenbrenner & Morris, 1998), children are nested within systems that include the child, family, school, community, and culture. The systems function independently and interactively to support or hinder a child's developmental progress.

Pianta was a pioneer in exploring how teachers and students impact upon each other within these systems. His Contextual Systems Model (Pianta & Walsh, 1996) asserts that although parent-child relationships are at the core of the family system, the teacher-student relationship is central to the classroom system.

The affective dimensions of teacher-student relationships, especially as they relate to young children, include closeness, conflict, and dependency (Pianta, 1999). Closeness is the degree of warmth and openness. Conflict involves the lack of rapport and negativity that manifests itself in discordant and coercive interactions. Dependency refers to overly dependent and clingy behaviors of the child.

Positive teacher-student relationships are characterized as high in closeness and low in conflict and dependency (Pianta, 1999). In their review of the related literature, Sabol and Pianta (2012) credit positive teacher-student relationships with enhancing children's prosocial skills, including raising their level of motivation and school engagement. Reducing student aggressive and anxious behavior is also attributed to teacher sensitivity in developing and maintaining positive relationships with students.

Like all meaningful relationships, teacher-student relationships take time to develop and are colored by the openness and reciprocity of each member of the dyad. Warmth and affection are comfortably expressed and received within positive relationships.

True responsivity affords understanding, validation, and caring (Reis & Gable, 2015). Verbal and nonverbal behaviors by the caregiver demonstrate that one's core self is understood and appreciated. Concern for one's well-being also is important.

Attachment theory offers insights into how close dyadic relationships develop (Ainsworth, 1989). An attachment relationship is designed to protect and support individuals when they feel threatened. To regain a sense of security and safety, individuals naturally seek protection from their attachment figure. Trust develops when a caregiver is available and responsive when needed.

As first explicated by Bowlby (1969), the early relationships babies have with their caregivers, particularly their mothers, create an internal working model that automatically operates throughout the lifespan and deeply affects subsequent relationships. Babies who have nurturing caregivers internalize that they are loved. They trust that their primary caregivers will be available to meet their needs. As a result, babies gravitate toward their caregivers when stressed or when they feel the need for support or comfort.

The majority of children have a strong attachment to their parents. When they begin school, they extend their positive internal working models to their teachers. As a result, they are ready and eager to engage with their teachers. In such optimal situations, teachers are appropriately regarded as "ad hoc" attachment figures (Verschueren & Koomen, 2012).

The relationships that teachers have with students who had secure attachments with their parents can be mutually satisfying and meaningful. They also can provide children with a secure base for greater exploration—encouraging them to take on the challenges associated with fulfilling their goals and aspirations (Feeney & Collins, 2015).

Positive teacher-student relationships are advantageous in many other ways. Higher student academic achievement is associated with supportive teacher relationships. This generalization is supported in a meta-analysis by Cornelius-White (2007) of nearly 1,000 studies conducted over 56 years. He concluded that positive teacher-student relationships have a greater impact on children's academic achievement ($r = 0.36$) than do educational innovations such as cognitive, affective, and behavioral programs ($r = 0.20$). In addition, children are more engaged at school and better able to communicate with their teachers when they have supportive relationships with them (O'Connor & McCartney, 2007).

CHILDREN AT RISK FOR CONFLICTUAL RELATIONSHIPS WITH THEIR TEACHERS

Not all teacher-student relationships are positive. Students whose early primary caregivers were negligent or emotionally distant bring those stances into their relationships with their teachers. They automatically replicate the same behavioral patterns with their teachers that they had with their early caregivers, even if those interactions were unsatisfying and counterproductive. Understandably, teachers encounter challenges when attempting to relate to children whose early attachment figures did not provide warm and trusting relationships.

Children with insecure relationships with their early caregivers often have adjustment problems during elementary school because they lack the type of internal working model that fosters self-regulation (O'Connor et al., 2012). Instead, they exhibit externalizing behaviors such as being aggressive with their peers or being noncompliant to their teacher's directives. Other children may be internalizers and may feel anxious, unengaged, or even depressed.

Teachers want their students to do well in school. When students are disruptive or unengaged in learning, many teachers feel angry or frustrated (Hagenauer et al., 2015). Conflict between the student and the teacher often occurs which further exacerbates the behavioral problems of the student (Spilt et al., 2012). For example, in one study, children who had externalizing and internalizing behavior problems in first grade and who had high levels of conflict and low levels of closeness with their teachers had even more serious adjustment problems by sixth grade (Collins et al., in press).

The repercussions of having a conflictual relationship with a teacher can be long lasting. Unsatisfying relationships with teachers can lead to children having negative perceptions of themselves and other adults; they may also establish negative patterns of interaction that can affect their intimate relationships when they are older (Collins et al., in press). Children cannot, by themselves, break away from such a negative trajectory of conflictual relationships. Only a responsive and caring adult, such as a teacher, can alter a child's perceptions of relationships with adults.

HOW RESPONSIVE TEACHERS CAN MAKE A DIFFERENCE FOR CHILDREN WITH INSECURE ATTACHMENTS

Fortunately, since Bowlby (1969) first offered his groundbreaking attachment theory, subsequent research has shown that early internal working models, while important, can be changed. Children who have insecure attachments with their mothers can benefit greatly if they have a warm and caring relationships with their teachers (O'Connor et al., 2012).

Some teachers are so warm and skilled that they can transcend the difficulties such children present. A sensitive and responsive relationship with a teacher can be healing because it provides a child with a safe haven at school (Verschueren & Koomen, 2012).

A safe haven at school offers an alternative comforting environment that buffers stressful situations by offering acceptance and reassurance (Feeney & Collins, 2015). Moreover, the security and safety afforded by the teacher who allows a child with externalizing or internalizing problems to test out new behaviors and patterns of interactions can lead to more adaptive social skills (Berry & O'Connor, 2010). As importantly, it assures the child that adults can be caring and trustworthy.

Most studies on teacher-student relationships have been descriptive, not experimental. More research is needed to identify how teachers can reduce the externalizing and internalizing behavior problems of students at risk of developing more serious disorders as they get older. An exception is the evidence-based *Responsive Classroom* program, which focuses on enhancing teacher-student relationships (Table 2.1).

Table 2.1   An Evidence-Based Intervention that Emphasizes Relationships: Responsive Classroom®

Summary of the program	*Responsive Classroom®* is an approach to elementary teaching that emphasizes social, emotional, and academic growth in a strong and safe school community.
Goal	The goal is to enable optimal student learning.
Target audience	Elementary schools
Theory of change	Children learn best when academic and social learning are fully integrated. Guiding Principles: • The social curriculum is as important as the academic curriculum. • How children learn is as important as what they learn. • The greatest cognitive growth occurs through social interaction. • To be successful academically and socially, children need a set of social skills: cooperation, assertion, responsibility, empathy, and self-control. • Knowing the children we teach—individually, culturally, and developmentally—is as important as knowing the content we teach. • Knowing the families of the children we teach and working with them as partners is essential to children's education.
Strategies offered	• Classroom practices: Morning meeting; Rule creation, Interactive modeling; Positive teacher language; Logical consequences; Guided discovery; Academic choice; Classroom organization, Working with families; Collaborative problem-solving. • School-wide practices: Aligning policies and procedures with *Responsive Classroom* philosophy; Allocating resources to support implementation; Planning all-school activities to build a sense of community; Welcoming family and community as partners; Organizing the physical environment.
Mode of delivery	The program is teacher led. Typically teachers and administrators attend an introductory week-long institute to learn about the first five practices. They attend a second week-long institute to learn about five additional practices after practicing the first set of strategies.
Materials/ curriculum	Books, DVDs, an assessment tool, and other materials may be purchased from the website. A number of related print materials are free including a quarterly newsletter.
Abstract	A quasi-experimental study was conducted with 3 intervention and 3 control schools. Approximately half of the students were minority and about a third were eligible for free or reduced lunch.
Results	*Fidelity of Implementation:* Teacher self-report and classroom observation compared the schools on the use of *Responsive Classroom* strategies. *Evidence Reported:* After controlling for poverty and previous test scores, *Responsive Classroom* had a small effect on reading and a small to medium effect on math for students who were in the program for more than one year. Based on self-reports and observations, large effects were found in implementing the related practices among teachers in the *Responsive Classroom* intervention compared to those in the control group.
Reference	Rimm-Kaufman, S. E., Fan, X., Chiu, Y. I., & You, W. (2007). The contribution of the Responsive Classroom approach on children's academic achievement: Results from a three year longitudinal study. *Journal of School Psychology, 45,* 401–421.
Developer	Northeast Foundation for Children, Inc.
Website	www.responsiveclassroom.org

CHANGES IN STUDENTS' RELATIONSHIPS
WITH THEIR TEACHERS OVER TIME

Like all relationships, teacher-student relationships are not static. Instead, they change over the course of a school year—either by growing closer or becoming more conflictual. At the beginning of the academic year, it is particularly important for teachers to be responsive to children who are dependent and who seek frequent reassurance. If teachers are nurturing and patient with them, the insecure patterns of behavior decrease over time (Verschueren & Koomen, 2012).

Changes in teacher-student relationships are also related to the types of instruction teachers provide their students. Teachers who provide more emotional support to their students early in the academic year promote higher-order thinking skills and language skills over the course of the year (Curby et al., 2013). The same type of teaching strategies also enhances progressively closer relationships between the teacher and students as the year progresses.

As children advance through elementary school, appropriate developmental changes result in changes in their relationships with their teachers. Most children become more independent and socially adept as they get older. Consequently, the role of a teacher involves less caregiving (O'Connor et al., 2011).

Although older students still value support from their teachers, relationships with peers increasingly become important (Sabol & Pianta, 2012). In addition, the world of older elementary school children rapidly expands beyond the immediacy of the classroom.

Children in the upper grades in elementary school usually have more adults to interact with at school and in the community. For example, they may have multiple teachers, or coaches, or music instructors. Still, teachers in the upper grades play an important role in the lives of their students. Children particularly value those teachers with whom they have more contact and are more likely to have closer relationships with them (Hagenauer et al., 2015).

Emotional support from teachers is particularly important when children face academic challenges in the upper grades. Older students are more engaged in their schoolwork if they perceive their teachers as supportive (Rimm-Kaufman et al., 2015). In addition, positive relationships with teachers are associated with reductions in externalizing behavior and, to a lesser degree, internalizing problems, as children get older (O'Connor et al., 2011).

OTHER IMPLICATIONS OF TEACHER-STUDENT RELATIONSHIPS

Children are astute observers of their teachers. They interpret their teachers' overt and nonverbal behaviors as signals revealing which students a teacher particularly likes or dislikes (Mercer & DeRosier, 2010). Even when a teacher's relationship with a particular student improves over the course of an academic year, negative perceptions of the child linger. Although children easily recognize an increase in conflict between a teacher's and a fellow student, they are less able to ascertain when a teacher has become more supportive of a child. In other words, children are more acutely aware of negative interactions with teachers than positive ones.

When students see conflict between a classmate and their teacher, it negatively influences their perceptions of the child (Elledge et al., 2015). The reverse can also be true. Teachers can play a protective role for children who are disliked by their classmates. A positive teacher relationship with a student who is disliked or rejected by their peers attenuates the risk that the child will become victimized by his or her classmates at a later time. After all, it is the teacher who role models how individuals should interact with each other in the classroom and within the larger school community.

Positive relationships with parents of students also are important. Responsivity extended to a child's parents can facilitate the resolution of a student's problematic behavior such as neglecting to complete homework. Likewise, respectful interactions with colleagues and administrators demonstrate how adults effectively collaborate in the best interests of children.

LOOKING AT TEACHER-STUDENT RELATIONSHIPS FROM A TEMPERAMENT LENS

Temperament theory poses a different perspective on teacher-student relationships by emphasizing how children respond differently to adults and their classroom environment. Temperament is the consistent reaction style that a child demonstrates across a variety of settings and situations, particularly in those that involve stress or change (McClowry, 2014). Temperament also is a social processing system through which children view and interact with the world—both altering the responses of others and contributing toward their own development.

Teachers tend to have close and nonconflictual relationships with students whose temperaments are conscientious and agreeable (Zee et al., 2013). Not all students, however, have those personality attributes. Many teachers have conflicts with students whose temperaments are high in motor activity or who are easily frustrated (Rudasill et al., 2010).

Other teachers, however, develop a supportive relationship with temperamentally challenging students and have a major impact on them. The students' academic outcomes are enhanced and their off-task and disruptive behavior is reduced (McCormick et al., 2015).

Children who are temperamentally shy also are challenging for many teachers. Shy children are reticent to initiate interactions with their teachers. In turn, teachers are less likely to engage with shy children (Rudasill & Rimm-Kaufman, 2009).

Appropriate responsiveness on a teacher's part, however, can enhance the adjustment of shy children. On the other hand, over reliance on a teacher can lead to fewer social interactions with peers and increase the social anxiety shy children often experience (Arbeau et al., 2010). Instead, teachers should support shy children in enhancing their social and emotional skills with their classmates and with adults (Coplan & Rudasill, 2016).

A comprehensive exploration of student temperaments, those that are challenging and those that are easy, can be found in *Temperament-Based Elementary Classroom Management* (McClowry, 2014). The book also provides more details about the evidence-based intervention, *INSIGHTS into Children's Temperament,* which is introduced in Table 2.2.

Chapter 2

Table 2.2   An Evidence-Based Temperament Intervention: INSIGHTS into Children's Temperament

Summary of the program	*INSIGHTS into Children's Temperament* (*INSIGHTS*) is a comprehensive intervention that enhances the social-emotional development and academic learning of young children and the behavior management skills of their teachers and parents.
Goals	The goals of *INSIGHTS* are to enhance classroom management and parenting skills by assisting teachers and parents in using temperament-based strategies that improve child behavior and academic skills. A related goal is to enhance children's ability to self-regulate.
Target audience	Kindergarten to second-grade students and their teachers and parents.
Theory of change	The intervention assists teachers and parents in recognizing how differences in children's behavior are often related to their temperament/personality. Then they learn how to match the behavioral strategies they use to a child's particular temperament. Children also benefit from understanding that individuals differ in their reactions to daily-life situations due to their temperaments.
Strategies offered	Parent and Teacher Programs: • The 3Rs: Recognize, Reframe, and Respond • The 2Ss: Scaffold and Stretch • The 2Cs: Gain Compliance and Competence The Children's Program: • Enhance Empathy • Resolve Daily Dilemmas
Mode of delivery	The intervention is conducted in ten weekly sessions. Facilitators conduct the teacher and parent sessions in separate groups. Teachers join the facilitators in conducting the children's sessions in the classrooms during the same ten weeks.
Materials/curriculum	The curriculum includes videotaped vignettes, handouts for the teachers and parents, puppets, workbooks, and storyboards for the children.
Abstract	Twenty-two urban elementary schools serving low-income families were randomly assigned to *INSIGHTS* or a supplemental reading program that served as an attention-control condition. Data on 435 students in 122 classrooms were collected at five time points across kindergarten and first grade.
Results	*Fidelity of Implementation:* Facilitators followed a detailed manual. Parent and teacher sessions were videotaped and reviewed for coverage of content and effectiveness of facilitation. *Evidence Reported:* Children enrolled in *INSIGHTS* experienced significantly faster growth in math and reading achievement and sustained attention than children enrolled in the supplemental reading program. In addition, children in *INSIGHTS* evidenced decreases in behavior problems while children in the supplemental reading program demonstrated increases.
Reference	O'Connor, E. E., Cappella, E., McCormick, M. P, & McClowry, S. G. (2014). An examination of the efficacy of *INSIGHTS* in enhancing the academic learning context. *Journal of Educational Psychology, 106,* 265–288. doi: 10.1037/a0036615.
Developer	Sandee McClowry, PhD, RN, FAAN
Website	www.insightsintervention.com

TEACHER ACTIONS THAT SUPPORT POSITIVE
TEACHER-STUDENT RELATIONSHIPS

There are many strategies teachers can use to develop and maintain positive relationships with their students. Teacher actions that build positive relationships with students are the same ones espoused in person-centered teaching approaches (Cornelius-White, 2007). They include being empathic and warm and encouraging student-initiated activities that foster critical thinking.

A critical component of emotionally supportive relationships is the way the individuals speak to each other. The recommended amount of positive to negative feedback that teachers should provide children is 5 to 1, respectively (Flora, 2000). Coincidentally, that same ratio is found in satisfying adult relationships (Gottman and Levinson, 1992).

The responsivity that empathic teachers relay to children entails sincerity coupled with self-awareness (Cornelius-White, 2007). Invariably, teachers will find it easier to relate to some children compared to others. Teachers judge their students more positively when they have similar personalities (Rausch et al., 2015).

Teachers need to be reflective so that they can accurately identify their emotional reactions and behaviors toward their students. More than two-thirds of teachers' judgments of their students are not related to student performance but to their teacher's perceptions (Südkamp et al., 2012). Self-awareness can lead to more objective perceptions and actions. Before they can improve a relationship with a student, teachers need to reframe more positively how they perceive the child (Spilt et al., 2012). Understanding the child's temperament and home situation is likely to prompt more empathy and fewer unintentional negative interactions.

Teacher-student relationships, like all relationships, require effort. As explored in this chapter, positive teacher-student relationships have indisputable benefits for children. Teachers also gain; teachers who have positive relationships with their students experience more joy, and less anger, anxiety, and work-related stress (Hagenauer et al., 2015). In other words, everyone wins!

SUMMARY

Close, positive relationships have an enduring effect on individuals throughout their lives. Although the relationships that children first have with their parents have a lasting impact, elementary school teachers have the potential to offer meaningful relationships to their students as well. Warm and caring teacher-student relationships are associated with higher student academic, social, and emotional outcomes.

A responsive relationship with a teacher is particularly important for children whose early caregivers' interactions were emotionally distant or neglectful. Children who had an insecure attachment with their primary caregivers often have behavioral issues at school.

Teachers are challenged to have a responsive relationship with students who have behavior problems. If, however, a teacher can transcend the difficulties imposed by a child's maladaptive behavior, healing can occur. The child experiences a safe haven at school, which can lead to more socially competent behavior and better relationship skills.

As children advance through elementary school, their need for supportive teachers continues, even though it changes. Older children are usually engaged with multiple adults at school and in the community. As a result, students often have less dependency on their classroom teacher. Yet, supportive relationships with teachers are still valued by older children.

Another way to examine teacher-student relationships is through a temperament lens. Classroom behavior and interactions are influenced by the temperaments of students. Children whose temperaments are high in activity or who are easily frustrated or are shy often challenge teachers' ability to relate positively to them. Teacher actions that include empathy and fostering students' critical thinking and initiative can, however, lead to better academic and social outcomes for all children.

CLASS DISCUSSION

- Do you remember a teacher who was particularly meaningful to you? Describe that teacher and explain why he or she made an impact on you.
- Make a list of specific actions that teachers can use to develop or maintain positive teacher-student relationships.

ASSIGNMENTS

Role-play one of these scenarios:
- Bridget is being unkind to another girl in your class. You reprimand her and she bursts into tears. What do you do?
- Paul is hesitant to participate in class. When you call on him, he barely answers your questions. However, Paul's written work indicates he understands the content. What do you do?
- Celia has been a cooperative student. Recently, however, her behavior has changed. She is not completing her homework and is aggressive on the playground? What do you do?

RECOMMENDED READINGS

McClowry, S. G. (2014). *Temperament-Based Elementary Classroom Management.* Lanham, MD: Rowman & Littlefield.

O'Connor, E., Collins, B., & Supplee, L. (2012). Behavior problems in middle childhood: The roles of maternal attachment and teacher-child relationships. *Attachment and Human Development, 14*(3), 265–288.

Sabol, T. J., & Pianta, R. C. (2012). Recent trends in research on teacher–child relationships. *Attachment & Human Development, 14*(3), 213–231. doi:10.1080/14616734.2012.672262.

Chapter 3

Classroom Organization

The way a classroom is organized makes a real difference in students' behavior and academic achievement. Think of classroom organization as setting the stage for academic productivity and social interactions. For example, let us peek into the classrooms of Mrs. Richards, a kindergarten teacher, and Ms. Morgan, who teaches fifth grade. Both teachers are anticipating the beginning of the school year.

If we were to observe their classrooms during the first weeks of school, we would find that Ms. Morgan effectively prepares her classroom and, consequently, her students are off to a good start. Mrs. Richards, unfortunately, duplicates the habits of less skilled teachers. The lack of organization at the beginning of the school will compromise classroom throughout the school room.

No doubt, you desire to be like Ms. Morgan in organizing your classroom. Fortunately, there are evidence-based strategies that you can apply. In this chapter:

- The relationship between organization and classroom management is explored.
- Three principles of classroom organization are discussed.
- The Response to Intervention (RtI) framework is offered as a way of matching students with three tiers of behavioral intervention. An evidence-based intervention from each of the tiers is presented:
  - *Positive Action®*, a Tier 1 classroom-wide program is aimed at supporting the social-emotional development of all students;
  - *Check, Connect, and Expect,* a Tier 2, is intended for students who require more intervention, which is delivered in small groups; and
  - *Prevent, Teach, and Reinforce,* a Tier 3 intervention, is an individualized model for treating students with severe behavior problems.
- An intervention directed at enhancing teacher skills, the *Classroom Organization and Management Program*, is presented.
- Practical evidence-based strategies are included for classroom organization in Appendix B at the end of the chapter.

ORGANIZATION IS ESSENTIAL TO GOOD
CLASSROOM MANAGEMENT

Preservice teachers often think that organizing the classroom environment involves distinctly different activities than those intended to establish and maintain good teacher-student relationships (Weinstein, 1998). Students, however, view these two components of classroom management as seamlessly intertwined. When children describe their preferences for teachers, they use words like, "warm," "engaged," and "organized." They perceive such teachers as creating a safe environment that is conducive to learning.

Evidence supports that the opinions of children about their teachers are right on target. Student achievement is higher in classrooms with teachers who are warm, engaging, and well organized (Cameron et al., 2008). Observational studies have also identified how skilled teachers like Ms. Morgan, compared to those like Ms. Richards, organize their classrooms in relation to materials and procedures, physical space, and time. The following three principles help to clarify those distinctions.

Principle #1: Classroom Organization Involves Teacher Planning and Student Practice

A substantial difference exists at the beginning of the school year between skilled and unskilled teachers (Cameron et al., 2008). The contrasts become even greater as the year progresses. Skilled teachers, like Ms. Morgan, expend a great deal of energy prior to the first day of class preparing their classroom for their new students. They develop procedures that will assure the children's safety and comfort. They also prepare packets for the students' parents that explain the classroom organizational procedures with suggestions on how parents can support their child in developing good study habits.

In the early days of the school year, effective teachers introduce their students to the classroom's procedures (Kern & Clemens, 2007). For example, they demonstrate how noninstructional activities, like collecting permission slips, will be handled. They also have the children practice how to safely navigate within the classroom and throughout the school building.

A number of mechanisms can be implemented to assist students in developing good organizational habits. Each student should have assigned locations for his or her various personal materials. Cubbies work well for younger children while folders are more appropriate for older students. Regardless of grade, posting daily and weekly schedules helps students track the classroom activities.

Principle #2: Organized Classrooms Maximize Their Resources

Prior to the beginning of the school year is how to arrange the physical layout of their classrooms. The ultimate goal is to create a classroom environment that engages students and, yet, is flexible enough to accommodate different types of activities. At the same time, care needs to be taken to assure that the physical environment is not so overstimulating that it becomes a distraction to the students.

Some layouts are better for supporting some classroom activities compared to others. Rows have a number of advantages. Attention to academic content is increased when students are seated in rows (Wheldall & Lam, 1987). Not surprisingly, disruptive students particularly benefit from seating in rows. The classroom layout also affects teachers. When students are seated in rows, teachers tend to provide more positive and less negative feedback.

Whole-class instruction with students in rows, however, is not ideal under all circumstances. A different room arrangement is needed to engage students in small group assignments. Likewise, teacher-students relationships are fostered when more informal small group arrangements are used.

Regardless of the classroom layout, teacher presence makes a difference (Fifer, 1986). When teachers are in the front of the classroom, students in the back of the room tend to be more disruptive. If, however, a teacher walks around the classroom, student behavior improves.

Principle #3: Time Organization Can Increase Student Engagement

One of the most powerful resources teachers have is *time*. The way a teacher utilizes time will determine how actively engaged students are in their classroom activities (Baker et al., 2008). Used well, time engages students at their optimal level.

The pace of instruction is important. By keeping the classroom momentum fast paced, teachers signal their expectations for classroom engagement. A great deal of instructional time can be lost while transitioning between activities (Codding & Smyth, 2008). Lengthy transitions disrupt classroom momentum.

Students are more engaged when teachers move right into a new task rather than beginning an activity with a motivational talk (Brophy et al., 1983). Instead, the recommended way to transition from one activity to another is to move quickly with deliberate starts and stops (Kern & Clemens, 2007). Teachers should announce a definite end to one activity, provide a short pause, gain the attention of the students, and then immediately start a new activity.

Skilled teachers also hold students accountable for completing work in the allotted time. They remind students how much time remains for an activity, schedule sessions to review the students' work while in progress, and provide immediate feedback regarding its quality (Kern & Clemens, 2007). Checklists help students keep track of their progress by specifying what tasks remain.

A guaranteed path to student boredom is an assignment that is too easy. Moderate difficulty increases engagement. Optimal engagement, or "flow," occurs when a student who is highly skilled is challenged to reach an even higher proficiency level (Shernoff & Csikszentmihalyi, 2009). When flow occurs, students experience high concentration and pleasure in a learning activity which, in turn, advances their skills to an even higher level.

Implementing a variety of teaching modalities also affects student engagement. Offering students choices in selecting an assignment increases their interest. Providing learning units that are particularly timely is another way to increase student engagement as described in Textbox 3.1.

Textbox 3.1   A Sidebar on Health-Related Topics

Classroom organization is not complete until arrangements have been made to extend the classroom beyond its physical walls. Although there are a myriad of possible ways to broaden the classroom, two health-related topics—nutrition and environmental education—are particularly relevant. Children appreciate learning content at school that applies to their daily lives and has the potential to influence their families' habits.

As defined by the Institute of Medicine (2005), children's health is the "extent to which children are able or enabled to (a) develop and realize their potential, (b) satisfy their needs, and (c) develop the capacities that allow them to interact successfully with their biological, physical, and social environments."

Poor food habits and inadequate exercise compromise the health of children in the United States. Approximately 17% of children are obese with African American and Hispanic children having a higher incidence than those who are Caucasian or Asian (Ogden et al., 2014). Obesity also compromises the social and emotional development of children and is associated with disruptive behavior, poor social skills, and emotional symptoms (Zametkin et al., 2004).

Because weight-related health problems are so prevalent, schools are frequently used as a setting for intervention. Comprehensive healthy eating interventions include nutrition education, optimization of the school food environment, and physical activity (Johnson et al., 2012).

Classroom teachers can engage their students in meaningful activities on a smaller scale by teaching them about healthy food choices. One effective teaching strategy is to engage students in creating a garden and then eating what they grow (Parmer et al., 2009). Tasting the produce from their own class garden can change students' attitudes toward vegetables (Johnson et al., 2012).

A broader health-related topic involves environmental education, a topic that lends itself to hands-on experiences within and beyond the classroom. The overall goal of environmental education is to teach children to protect and conserve the environment by implementing sustainable practices (Liefländer et al., 2013). Children learn how they can contribute toward sustainability practices in their classrooms, in their homes, and in the larger community. Like all topics, environmental education is best taught when cognitive, attitudinal, and affective components are experienced and integrated.

Keeping students engaged requires a concerted effort by teachers when the classroom community includes students with varying academic abilities. To maximize student engagement, coursework needs to match a student's cognitive ability. For example, students who are gifted need considerable intellectual stimulation in order to stay engaged in their course assignments. They also have unique intellectual and social needs as discussed in Textbox 3.2.

If students are disengaged, classroom problems are guaranteed to happen. Not only do the children fail to achieve their academic potential, but disengaged students frequently exhibit behavior problems as well. Boredom in the classroom is a license for student misbehavior.

Textbox 3.2   An FYI: Meeting the Multifaceted Social and Emotional Needs of Gifted Students

Intellectually gifted pupils, with IQs of 120 or higher, often present their own challenges within the classroom community (Gagné, 2005). A myth purports that intellectually gifted students can make it "on their own" and do not need specialized support to reach their potential. Understandably, some teachers find it difficult to successfully teach their average students while simultaneously attending to the enrichment needs of their gifted pupils. As a result, most gifted students are often not adequately challenged in schools (Pfeiffer, 2012). Boredom with school compromises the intellectual potential of gifted children.

Gifted children often experience asynchronous or uneven levels of development (Robinson, 2012). Teachers and parents may have unrealistic expectations about gifted children and expect them to be as socially mature as they are intellectually. Instead, gifted children lag in their social development.

Several factors contribute to their asynchronous development. To seek out individuals with similar intellectual levels, gifted children frequently seek out the company of older children or even adults. In addition, students who have been accelerated are with classmates who are older than themselves. As a result, gifted children are less skilled when dealing with their age-appropriate peers. Rejection from less intellectually advanced peers creates a sense of feeling different. Often, gifted children feel isolated or without a true peer group.

Despite the challenges inherent in asynchronous development, the majority of gifted children are well adjusted (Pfeiffer, 2012). Their unique social, emotional, and career development needs, however, warrant specialized supportive services. Many gifted children are perfectionists, emotionally intense, and highly sensitive (Daniels & Piechowski, 2008). In addition, they often feel a great deal of pressure to perform at extremely high levels and may experience symptoms of depression. Exceptionally gifted children, with IQs over 150, are more likely to have adjustment problems than those who are moderately gifted (Robinson, 2012).

Gifted children benefit from counseling that takes their social-emotional development in account (Hébert & Kelly, 2006). Another need of gifted children is for career counseling because they often have specific career goals at a much younger age than most children. In addition, the parents of gifted children can benefit from support so that they can better understand the multifaceted needs of their gifted children. Of particular concern is helping families achieve a balance lifestyle for the gifted child and for the family as a whole.

Despite their high IQs, some gifted children are nonachievers. Like all students, school services should be offered to gifted children who are not progressing appropriately. Testing may be needed to determine whether a learning disability or emotional problem is compromising the student's academic achievement (Pfeiffer, 2012).

As presented throughout this book, a number of evidence-based classroom management interventions exist. The programs vary in their overall aims. Some are designed to prevent behavior problems from occurring.

Other evidence-based interventions aim to reduce or treat existing behavioral problems. Before selecting a classroom management intervention, it is important to match the program to the level of students' behavioral needs. In the following section, a framework is presented to guide in that process.

CLASSROOM MANAGEMENT STRATEGIES SHOULD BE MATCHED TO STUDENT'S BEHAVIORAL NEEDS AS DEFINED BY THE PYRAMID MODEL

Teachers report that 65% of children in the United States begin kindergarten ready to learn (Boyer, 1991). Children who are ready for school have the academic and social building blocks necessary for learning and for successfully interacting with their teachers and classmates. Some of the early readiness skills include recognizing colors and the letters of the alphabet and counting.

Other readiness skills involve sitting still for short periods of time and listening attentively to a teacher. Getting along with one's classmates is also critical. Children who begin kindergarten with these skills will probably progress well in school if they receive quality evidence-based instruction from teachers who are adept at pedagogy and classroom management.

Many of the children who are not ready for school will develop academic or behavioral problems or both difficulties during elementary school. So will some of the children who were prepared. Regardless of their genesis, early academic and behavioral problems are likely to escalate over time if they are not remediated.

In recent years, educators have implemented a Response to Intervention (RtI) framework to catch students who are having difficulties early in their elementary

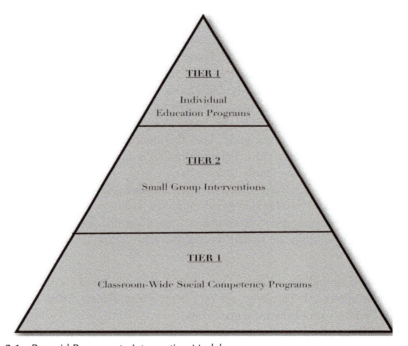

Figure 3.1   Pyramid Response to Intervention Model.

school years before they have a chance to fail. RtI is a systematic problem-solving framework for organizing and evaluating the effectiveness of different levels of evidence-based interventions (Fox et al., 2010). Although RtI is generally applied to academic achievement, the principles also apply to social and emotional behavior (Sailor et al., 2009).

When the RtI framework is fully applied, students receive an evidence-based classroom instruction that matches their particular needs. Changes in the relevant outcomes are carefully monitored using screening tools and standardized tests. The children who have a discrepancy between their current and appropriate level of performance are identified as "at-risk" and are provided additional services to remediate their problems. Changes in student performance are monitored. Lengthy transitions disrupt classroom momentum. If needed, adjustments are made so that the services continue to match the difficulties the students experience.

Like academic instruction, behavioral strategies should match a child's level of social and emotional development (Sugai et al., 2000). As shown in the Pyramid Model in Figure 3.1, behavioral interventions exist on three levels. Each tier builds upon the previous one. The differences between the tiers are in the specificity and intensity of the intervention and in the frequency of monitoring the child's responsiveness to the intervention (Fox et al., 2010).

Tier 1

Attending school requires that all children expand their ability to meet the ever broadening social competencies required in peer and adult interactions. As a proactive approach, every classroom should implement an evidence-based social and emotional learning program. The focus of such a class-wide intervention is to help students meet the developmentally appropriate demands of middle childhood such as making and maintaining friends and relating and negotiating with teachers and other adults. *Positive Action®*, an example of a Tier 1 social competency program, is highlighted in Table 3.1.

Tier 2

About 5%–15% of students are nonresponders to a Tier 1 classroom-wide social and emotional learning program. Many of students who are nonresponsive to Tier 1 classroom programs will benefit from a Tier 2 intervention (Fox et al., 2010).

The importance of providing more intensive intervention to these students cannot be overstated. Students who exhibit emotional or behavioral problems oftentimes become progressively worse. (Bradshaw et al., 2010). Tier 2 supplemental services aim at identifying a child's source of deficits and providing focused behavioral strategies to reduce them.

Tier 2 services are often delivered concurrently with the Tier 1 class-wide intervention. In addition to the Tier 1 classroom program, students assigned with Tier 2 services receive additional intervention with small groups of children who are exhibiting behavior problems. Typically, Tier 2 behavioral interventions last 8–12 weeks and are sometimes repeated for a second time. *Check, Connect, and Expect* is an example of an evidence-based Tier 2 intervention (Table 3.2).

Table 3.1   An Evidence-Based Intervention for a Tier 1 Intervention: Positive Action®

Summary of the program	The mission of *Positive Action®* program (PA) is to transform individuals, schools, families, and communities by teaching and reinforcing positive actions for a lifetime of health, happiness, and success. We define success and happiness as feeling good about who you are, what you do, and how you treat others.
Goals	The goal of PA is to offer a program that is effective, efficient, empowering, and easy to use. PA is an evidence-based program for improving academics, behavior, and character.
Target audience	Kindergarten through 12th grade.
Theory of change	Children learn best when academic and social learning are fully integrated.
Guiding principles	PA consists of five components. It works by teaching and reinforcing the intuitive philosophy that you feel good about yourself when you do positive actions; there is a positive way to do everything. The program teaches the positive actions for the physical, intellectual, social, and emotional areas of the self. The philosophy is illustrated by the Thoughts-Actions-Feelings Circle where positive thoughts lead to positive actions, positive actions lead to positive feelings about yourself, and positive feelings lead to more positive thoughts.
Strategies offered	The curriculum includes scripted lessons for classroom use, a school-wide climate program, and family- and community-involvement components.
	The first unit begins with the philosophy and Thoughts-Actions-Feeling, and units two through six explain key positive actions for the whole self or physical, intellectual, social, and emotional areas.
	Unit 1: Self-Concept. What It Is, How It's Formed, and Why It's Important (Philosophy and Circle)
	Unit 2: Positive Actions for your Body and Mind
	Unit 3: Managing Yourself Responsibly
	Unit 4: Treating Others the Way You Like to be Treated (Social Skills and Character)
	Unit 5: Being Honest with Yourself and Others (Mental Health)
	Unit 6: Improving Yourself Continually (Setting and Achieving Goals)
Mode of delivery	The materials are prepared so the content can be self-taught or individuals who conduct the program can attend workshops and/or receive follow-up training.
Materials/ curriculum	The materials are offered in a number of kits directed at specific grade levels. There are English and Spanish versions and kits for use in the community.
Abstract	A randomized trial of the effectiveness of PA took place in 20 public elementary schools on three Hawaiian islands. The study followed students who began the program as 1st or 2nd graders and received up to 4 years of the program. Schools were matched on a number of socio-demographic and school-related factors and then randomized into 10 intervention and 10 control schools. Fifth graders self-reported (N = 1714) on lifetime substance use, violence, and voluntary sexual activity, and teachers reported on student (N = 1225) substance use and violence.
Results	*Fidelity of Implementation:* The intervention was delivered by teachers who were trained and supported by project staff.
	Evidence Reported: Student reported substance use and violence were significantly lower among who had attended intervention schools. Sexual activity also was lower for intervention students. Teacher reports substantiated effects. Students exposed to the program for more than 3 years had significantly lower rates of all negative behaviors. The reduction of negative behaviors by almost half provides evidence that a comprehensive school-based program can have a substantial impact on reducing risk-related behaviors of young adolescents.
Reference	Beets, M. B., Flay, B. R., Vuchinich, S., Snyder, F. J., Acock, A., Li, K. Burns, K., Isaac J. Washburn, I. J., & Durlak, J. 2009). Use of a social and character development program to prevent substance use, violent behaviors, and sexual activity among elementary students in Hawaii. *American Journal of Public Health, 99*(8), 1438–1445. doi: 10.2105/AJPH.2008.142919
Developer	Carol Gerber Allred, PhD
Website	http://www.positiveaction.net/

Table 3.2 An Evidence-Based Intervention for a Tier 2 Intervention: Check, Connect, and Expect

Summary of the program	The *Check, Connect, and Expect (CCE)* intervention combines features from two programs, the *Check & Connect* and the *Behavior Education Program* to support students who require Tier 2 services for behavioral problems. The *CCE* intervention focuses on improving students' positive relationships and prosocial behavior via daily positive interactions with school staff, reinforcement for success, and immediate feedback for problem behavior.
Goal	The goal is for students to meet daily criteria for meeting school social expectations and to become a graduate of the CCE. Graduates then serve as peer mentors to help other students demonstrate positive social behavior throughout the school.
Target audience	Tier 2 students who meet the criteria for externalizing or internalizing behavior on the Systematic Screening for Behavior Disorders (Walker & Severson, 1990) and whose teachers agree would benefit from this daily program.
Theory of change	The *CCE* intervention is based on the theory that relationships with school staff, reinforcement of clear expectations and social behavior, and engagement in school contribute to students' academic and social outcomes.
Strategies offered	*CCE* includes (a) daily supervision, monitoring, and coaching; (b) frequent feedback on academic and social performance; (c) point systems based on social and academic goals; (d) reinforcement for meeting criteria on the goals; e) use of a positive adult role model; and (f) social skills instruction when necessary.
Mode of delivery	The intervention relies on an adult mentor, called a coach, to supervise, monitor, and provide feedback to the students at the beginning and end of a school day and during weekly meetings. Students check in and out daily and weekly using a Daily Progress Report (DPR) on which their specific behavioral goals are recorded and monitored. Classroom teachers also provide behavioral feedback throughout the day. The mentors chart and review the DPRs. Mentors hold problem-solving sessions with students when they do not meet their behavioral goals.
CCE includes five levels of intervention: Basic, Basic Plus, Intensive, Self-Monitoring, and Program Graduates. Students self-monitor as they advance in the intervention prior to graduating from the program.
Materials/ curriculum	A "Check-In and a Check-Out Adherence and Quality Form" and a number of other standardized tools are used to monitor the students' behavior.
Abstract	Eighteen socio-demographically similar schools were randomly assigned to *CCE* or to the comparison group. Teachers in the schools identified students in 1st to 3rd grade as at risk for social, behavioral, and/or academic failure. Over the course of the study, 323 students and 249 of their teachers participated in the study.
Results	*Fidelity of Implementation:* Treatment adherence and quality measures for coaches were consistent across the two years of the study with their check-in and check-out procedures meeting high levels for adherence and quality. Teacher's level of adherence decreased slightly for graduate group from year 1 to 2 (98%–92%) whereas their adherence to the program with CCE nongraduate group remained relatively constant (94%–95%) across the two years.
Evidence Reported: Among the 73 students who graduated from the CCE intervention, 60% remained in the normative behavioral range during the remaining two years of the study. The graduate group demonstrated significantly lower externalizing (disruptive or aggressive) and internalizing (depression or withdrawn) behavior after the intervention. The 48 nongraduates and 86 students in the comparison group remained at clinically at-risk levels.
Reference	Cheney, D. A., Stage, S. A., Hawken, L. S, Lynass, L., Mielenz, C., Waugh, M. (2009). A 2-year outcome study of the Check, Connect, and Expect Intervention for students at risk for severe behavior problems. *Journal of Emotional and Behavioral Disorders, 17,* 226–243. doi:10.1177/1063426609339186.
Developer	Douglas Cheney, Scott Stage, Leanne Hawken, Lori Lynass, Andrea Flower & Bridget Walker
Website	http://depts.washington.edu/chdd/ucedd/eeu_7/check_expect_7.html

Table 3.3   An Evidence-Based Intervention for a Tier 3 Intervention: The Prevent-Teach-Reinforce Model

Summary of the program	*Prevent-Teach-Reinforce* (PTR) is a team-based model that includes conducting a functional behavioral assessment, developing a behavior support plan that will **P**revent the occurrence of severe behavior problems. **T**each alternative skills, and **R**einforce student prosocial behaviors. The PTR model is implemented by the child's teacher and other members of the team with the support of a behavioral interventionist trained in behavioral analysis.
Goal	The goal of the PTR model is to reduce the occurrences of serious behavior problems, increase prosocial behavior, enhance academic engagement, and prevent referrals to special education or other restricted educational settings.
Target audience	Kindergarten to 8th-grade students who are exhibiting persistent challenging behaviors that are (1) disruptive, dangerous, or interfering, (2) incompatible with optimal learning, and (3) repeatedly resistant to routine school and classroom management procedures.
Theory of change	Schools can prevent serious student behavior problems from occurring by adjusting the curriculum and environment; teaching proactive communication skills; and reinforcing prosocial behavior and academic achievement.
Strategies offered	The PTR model includes 5 steps: (1) **Team building** among teachers, administrators, behavior experts, parents, and other members of the student's education team; (2) **Goal setting and data collection** to evaluate the status of the student's behavior and ensure shared priorities; (3) **Assessment** to understand the student's behavior problems and any influencing factors; (4) **Intervention** strategies that include effective individualized plans; and (5) **Evaluation** of the effects of the intervention.
Mode of delivery	Individually applied to the children with coaching provided to their teachers.
Materials/ curriculum	A standardized user-friendly manual is available. The manual includes a CD-ROM with all of the printable forms and tools needed to implement PTR including behavior support plan templates and those related to a Functional Behavioral Assessment.
Abstract	Two hundred forty-five kindergarten to 8th-grade students with serious behavior problems were randomly assigned to the PTR model or to the usual services their school offered.
Results	*Fidelity of Implementation:* Fidelity was conducted by direct observation of teachers' adherence to the core components of the intervention and for the quality of their implementation. Almost all of the teachers implemented the intervention with high fidelity. *Evidence Reported:* After the intervention, the students in PTR exhibited fewer behavioral problems, had better social skills, and were more academically engaged than the children who received the typical school services.
Reference	Iovannone, R., Greenbaum, P. E., Wang, W., Kincaid, D., Dunlap, G., & Strain, P. (2009). Randomized controlled trial of the Prevent-Teach-Reinforce tertiary intervention for students with problem behaviors: Preliminary outcomes. *Journal of Emotional and Behavioral Disorders, 17*(4), 213–225.
Developer	The model was developed by Glen Dunlap, Rose Iovannone, Donald Kincaid, Kelly Wilson, Kathy Christiansen, Phillip Strain, and Carie English.
Website	http://www.brookespublishing.com/store/books/dunlap-70151/index.htm

Table 3.4 An Evidence-Based Intervention for Teacher Professional Development: Classroom Organization and Management Program (COMP)

Summary of the program	The *Classroom Organization and Management Program (COMP)* is a teacher professional development program.
Goals	*COMP*'s goals are to help teachers improve their overall instructional and behavioral management skills through planning, implementing, and maintaining effective classroom practices.
Target audience	Teachers in K-12th-grade classrooms.
Theory of change	Good classroom management is the foundation for quality instruction and student achievement, it requires an ongoing process of careful crafting and development through planning, implementation, and maintenance.
Strategies offered	Organizing the classroom 1. Planning and teaching rules and procedures 2. Managing student academic work 3. Maintaining good student behavior 4. Planning for instruction 5. Conducting instruction and maintaining momentum 6. Getting the year off to a good start
Mode of delivery	*COMP* is delivered initially in a one-week professional development program. Advanced training is also available.
Materials/ curriculum	Each of the seven key areas of classroom management training modules includes: – a self-assessment checklist – a summary of related research – suggestions of ideas that work – case studies for problem-solving – activities to help teachers apply ideas from key areas directly to the classroom
Abstract	Forty-six experienced teachers and their new teacher protégés from two school consortia were the participants in this quasiexperimental study. Half of the mentors attended a four-day *COMP* workshop. The others served as the comparison group. Assessment was conducted based on observations and self-reports.
Results	*Evidence Reported*: Protégés of mentors who participated in *COMP*, compared to those in the comparison group, showed evidence of developing and sustaining more workable classroom routines, managed instruction more smoothly, and gained student cooperation in academic tasks more effectively. Their students were also more engaged in schoolwork and had relatively less inappropriate or disruptive behavior.
Reference	Evertson, C. M., & Smithey, M. W. (2000). Mentoring effects on protégés' classroom practice: An experimental field study. *Journal of Educational Research, 93,* 294–304.
Developer	Carolyn M. Evertson, PhD
Website	www.comp.org

Tier 3

About 5% of students exhibit persistent and serious behavioral problems at school that are not resolved by Tier 2 interventions. As mandated in the amendments to the Individuals with Disabilities Education Act (IDEA, P. L. 105–170), these students should receive intensive individualized services strategically directed at their emotional and behavioral problems.

To determine the appropriate individualized services, a functional behavior assessment (FBA) is conducted, as will be discussed in more detail in chapter 6 (Sugai et al., 2000). The following evidence-based intervention, *The Prevent-Teach-Reinforce Model* has standardized the FBA process with tools that assess its implementation and to measure its effect on the student's behavior (Table 3.3).

SUPPORT FOR TEACHERS' CLASSROOM MANAGEMENT SKILLS

Prior to assessing a student for level 2 or level 3 behavioral services, it is critical to evaluate whether the student's teacher has adequate organizational and classroom management skills. If not, intervention is appropriately first directed at the teacher's classroom management skills. Support for teachers can come through consultation with more experienced teachers or professional development programs like the *Classroom Organization and Management Program*. A description of the program is presented in Table 3.4.

SUMMARY

This chapter presents three principles of classroom organization that influence students' academic achievement and behavior. Effective teachers spend time preparing their classroom and planning procedures before the academic year begins. The teachers also provide students with opportunities to practice the procedures during the first couple of weeks so that they become a routine part of the classroom.

Effective teachers also plan how they will use their available resources to configure the classroom layout. In general, highly structured classrooms foster student attentiveness and reduce disruptive behavior. Cluster desks or semicircles, however, support social interactions and group assignments.

Regardless of the physical arrangement of the classroom, optimal use of time enhances student engagement. Keeping the curriculum appropriately paced and matched to the student's intellectual abilities increases student engagement.

If student behavioral problems occur, social and emotional learning programs should be matched to the three tiers of the RtI framework. Tier 1 is intended for all students in a regular education classroom. Tier 2 involves the 5%–15% of students who are unresponsive to Tier 1. These interventions involve focused strategies, delivered in a small group format, that match the student's particular behavioral problems. About 5% of students with serious, persistent behavioral disorders require more intensive Tier 3 interventions.

Intervention can also be directed at teachers who need better classroom organization and management skills. In the next chapter, you will learn about other discipline and strategies that are intended to make your classroom a community of learners.

RELATED WEBSITES

- The Association for Positive Behavior Support:
  - http://www.apbs.org/
- Project REACH: The National Center for Students with Intensive Social, Emotional, and Behavioral Needs:
  - http://coe.lehigh.edu/research/national-center-students-intensive-social-behavioral-and-emotional-needs-project-reach

COURSE ASSIGNMENTS WITH CLASS DISCUSSION

- Arrange a schematic model of a classroom.
  - Discuss your rationale for your classroom design.
  - Plan a classroom routine that demonstrates how physical movement will occur in your classroom when lining up for lunchtime or moving to choice centers. Role-play practicing the routine with your colleagues acting as elementary school students.
- Prepare a developmentally appropriate drop-off box for your classroom that students can use to return communications from their parents.
- Review Appendix B at the end of this book for practical strategies that work for organizing a classroom.

RECOMMENDED READINGS

Colvin, G., Sugai, G., Good, R. H., & Lee, Y. (1997). Using active supervision and precorrection to improve transition behaviors in an elementary school. *School Psychology Quarterly. Special Issue: Changing Teacher and Staff Behavior to Benefit Children, 12*, 344–363. doi:10.1037/h0088967.

Sailor, W., Doolittle, J., Bradley, R., & Danielson, L. (2009). Response to Intervention and Positive Behavior Support. In W. Sailor, G. Dunlap, G. Sugai, & R. Horner (Eds.), *Handbooks of positive behavior support* (pp. 729–754). New York, NY: Springer.

Simonsen, B., Fairbanks, S., Briesch, A., Myers, D., & Sugai, G. (2008). Evidence-based practices in classroom management: Considerations for research to practice. *Education & Treatment of Children, 31*, 351–380.

Chapter 4

Student Discipline in the Context of a Community of Learners

A community is a group of individuals who share a common purpose and espouse a set of values essential to achieving their goals. Communities create a sense of belonging, acceptance, and mutual responsibility. Members of a genuine community know that they are appreciated for their unique characteristics and talents. Feeling valued sets the stage for mutually responsive interactions.

Although a community is comprised of individuals, it functions, ideally, as a cohesive whole. Each member relies on others to contribute to the well-being of the community. Support is offered when needed. In addition, well-articulated systems are in place to ensure fairness and safety.

Classrooms have the potential to form a special type of community—a community of learners. Respectful interactions and self-regulation are foundational for creating and maintaining a community of learners. Nevertheless, even when teachers and students do all they can to cultivate the classroom community, student misbehavior will occur.

When values are not respected or the mutually agreed-upon rules are not followed, fair and consistent discipline practices should follow. Depending on the severity of the student's misbehavior, different strategies are recommended. The results of research studies can inform teachers how to discipline from a community of learners' perspective.

In this chapter:

- The multifaceted benefits that students and teachers derive from forming a community of learners are explained.
- An evidence-based intervention, the *Caring School Community,* which aims to foster a community of learners, is presented.
- Recent research on classroom management is discussed.
- Two evidence-based interventions, *PATHS* and *Teaching Students to Be Peacemakers,* are described as examples of social and emotional learning programs.
- Major takeaways from classroom management research are presented.
- Five evidence-based guidelines for preventing student problem behavior are offered.
- *KiVa,* an evidence-based antibullying intervention, is highlighted.

THE MULTIFACETED BENEFITS TO CREATING
A COMMUNITY OF LEARNERS

Classrooms that engender a sense of community are advantageous for a number of reasons. Students are more motivated to learn when they feel that they are part of a community. As a result, academic achievement is higher, and the social and emotional development of students is enhanced because empathy, assertiveness, and collaboration are fostered (Schaps et al., 2004).

Teachers also benefit from a caring environment. They experience more job satisfaction and feel more efficacious in classroom management (Solomon et al., 1996). Table 4.1 describes the *Caring School Community,* an evidence-based intervention that focuses on strengthening the community of learners.

The creation of a community of learners does not happen spontaneously. Instead, it begins with teachers who take deliberate steps to support their students' intellectual, emotional, and moral growth individually and collectively. Creating and maintaining a community of learners entails engaging students as active learners, fostering mutual respect, monitoring student behavior, setting limits, teaching students alternative ways to behave, and responding decisively when serious behavior problems occur. Each component builds upon the others.

Sounds simple, doesn't it? Actually, managing student behavior and maintaining a classroom community that supports learning have challenged many generations of teachers (The New Teacher Project, 2013). In the first half of the twentieth century, without an organized body of knowledge to guide them, novice teachers relied on commonsense strategies passed on from their more experienced colleagues. Sometimes the advice worked, but often it did not. Another source of advice came from "experts," who recommended some forms of punishment now considered to be harsh, such as corporal punishment (Brophy, 2006).

Systematic research on classroom discipline began in the 1950s under the broader rubric of classroom management. Student discipline was regarded as one essential part of a broader construct that often incorporated other components, such as classroom organization and instruction (Martin et al., 2016).

Over the next 50 years, the studies on classroom management shifted between two approaches that still influence today's research (Bear, 2015):

1. How teachers and other adults can change student behavior.
2. How behavior problems can be prevented by enhancing student self-discipline.

RECENT RESEARCH ON CLASSROOM MANAGEMENT

Research on classroom management has flourished in the last 15 years (Emmer & Sabornie, 2015). Descriptive studies and experimental designs have yielded empirical support for the strategies and interventions presented throughout this book. Although there is some overlap, most of the recent classroom management research can be classified into three types: ecological, behavioral, and social and emotional learning approaches (Bear, 2015).

Table 4.1 An Evidence-Based Intervention for Building a Community of Learners: The Caring School Community

Summary of the program	*The Caring School Community* (CSC) is a program that builds classroom and the school-wide community, thereby, strengthening students' connectedness to school.
Goals	Four connectedness-building principles are at the heart of the *CSC* program: • Deliberately cultivate respectful, supportive relationships; • Provide frequent opportunities for collaboration; • Provide developmentally appropriate opportunities for autonomy and influence; and • Emphasize common purposes and ideals.
Target audience	Kindergarten through 6th grade.
Theory of change	Schools can and do make a difference in how students develop as citizens and as whole people. Students who feel connected to their school perform better academically, and are less likely to engage in problem behaviors. • Children thrive in caring school and classroom communities. • Children learn better when their basic psychological needs are met—their needs for experiencing autonomy, belonging, competence, and emotional safety. • Students' sense of connectedness to school affects their aspirations, motivation, and behavior. • A steady diet of competitive situations makes learning more difficult.
Strategies offered	The program's four components support the learning of intrapersonal and interpersonal skills and strengthening of prosocial motivation: • Class meetings • Cross-age buddies program • Homeside activities • School-wide activities
Mode of delivery	Teachers learn how to deliver the program through use of detailed implementation materials and tailored types and levels of professional development. Training-of-trainers is also available for school or district-level leaders and coaches.
Materials/ curriculum	Teacher packages for Grades K–6 include Class Meeting Lesson Kits, Teacher's Calendar, Homeside Activities, School-wide Community-Building Activities, Cross-Age Buddies Activity Book, and Caring School Community Overview. A principal set includes all of the teacher materials. Related Read Aloud libraries also are available.
Abstract	A longitudinal follow-up study was conducted with 1,246 middle school students who had participated in a study that tested the efficacy of the *Child Development Project* (which was the precursor to the *Caring School Community*) when they were in elementary school. The children had attended twelve schools, six of which were comparison schools that did not receive any intervention, three schools that had high implementation of the intervention and three schools with low implementation.
Evidence Reported	Students who were in the program in elementary school compared to those who were in comparison schools, had more positive relations with their teachers, and liked school more, had greater sense of efficacy, and were more engaged in positive youth activities. Their teachers reported that they were also less withdrawn than those in the comparison schools. The effects were greater in high-implementation schools. Among the many findings were that those students had a greater sense of community, higher academic performance, and were more prosocial and less antisocial than comparison students.
References	Battistich, V., Schaps, E., & Wilson, N. (2003). Effects of an elementary school intervention on students' "connectedness" to school and social adjustment during middle school. *Journal of Primary Prevention, 24*, 243–262.
Developer	The Developmental Studies Center
Website	http://www.devstu.org/page/caring-school-community

Ecological Approaches

The emphasis in ecological approaches is on the teacher actions that prevent student behavior problems from occurring in the first place (Doyle, 2006). The ultimate goal of the ecological approach is for teachers to foster their students' self-regulation. Teachers reason with their students and encourage them to make prosocial decisions (Hickey & Schafer, 2006). Classroom rules and procedures are developed with student input. When students do not follow them, teachers intervene quickly, consistently, and fairly.

Another component of ecological approaches is that way that teachers talk to their students (Wallace et al., 2014). In his book, *Choice Words: How Our Language Affects Children's Learning,* Johnston (2004) explains that "teacher talk" transmits more than content. Words relay teachers' perceptions of their students and the quality of their relationships. Positive teacher communication also encourages students to develop new identities. Textbox 4.1 presents "teacher talk" examples from Johnston's book.

TextBox 4.1   Some Examples of Positive Teacher Talk

Addressing students as active learners:
- Did anyone notice?
- I see you know how to begin.
- Write down the answer you wished you had written.
- How did you figure that out?
- What part do you understand and what part are you not sure about?

Inviting students to take on new or more positive identities
- What a talented young . . . you are.
- I bet you are proud of yourself.

Behavioral Approaches

In contrast, the behavioral approach focuses on the direct teacher actions that change student behavior (Bear, 2015). The goals of the behavioral approach are to teach students new behaviors and to strengthen existing ones. Or teachers may strive to weaken or stop behaviors that already exist.

To improve children's behaviors, teachers reward those that are desirable and punish undesirable ones (Payne, 2015). When strategies from the behavioral approach are correctly applied, undesirable behaviors are expected to fade away. More details about the principles of behaviorism are presented in chapter 6.

Behavioral strategies can be applied to individual students, to the classroom as a whole, or can be implemented schoolwide. A notable evidence-based class-wide intervention, the *Good Behavior Game*, is presented in Table 4.2. Table 4.3 describes the *School-Wide Positive Behavioral Support* approach.

Social and Emotional Learning

A third approach, social and emotional learning, underlies a number of recently developed evidence-based interventions. Social and emotional learning focuses on

Table 4.2   An Evidence-Based Behavioral Intervention: The Good Behavior Game

Summary of the program	The Good Behavior Game (GBG) is a team-based token economy that encourages students to inhibit inappropriate classroom behavior.
Goal	Reduce student disruptive and off-task behavior, drug abuse, delinquency, and other problem outcomes; promote self-regulation and positive social relationships.
Target audience	Elementary through high school
Theory of change	Positive peer pressure is used to reducing students' negative behavior so that they can be more engaged in academic instruction.
Strategies offered	Students in a classroom are assigned to teams that are heterogeneous for gender, behavior, and academic achievement. Teachers define the classroom rules and work with students to identify the behaviors that support the rules and those that constitute infractions of the rules. When the game is played, a team receives a check mark when one of the members exhibits an infraction of the rules. Teams with four or fewer check marks win the game and receive a reward. All teams can win. In the beginning of the year, the game is played three times a week for ten minutes a day. Over the course of the school year, the game is played for longer periods of time and, during different times of the day. Rewards evolve from being tangible and delivered immediately to being intangible and delivered on a delayed scheduled to support generalization of positive behaviors.
Mode of delivery	GBG is implemented by classroom teachers who use the strategy during regular instruction.
Materials/ curriculum	Training and support are offered by the American Institutes for Research.
Abstract	The first randomized clinical trial examining the efficacy of GBG was conducted in first- and second-grade classrooms in Baltimore public schools beginning in the 1985–1986 school year.
Results	Compared to the children in the control group, GBG was effective in reducing the first- and second-grade student's off-task (Brown, 1993) and disruptive behavior (Dolan et al., 1993). In a longitudinal follow-up after 15 years, the young adults who were in classrooms that "played" GBG when they were in first and second grade, compared to the control group, had fewer psychiatric problems and less drug and alcohol abuse (Kellam et al., 2008).
References	Brown, C. H. (1993). Analyzing preventive trials with generalized additive models [Special issue]. *American Journal of Community Psychology, 21,* 635–664. Dolan, L. J., Kellam, S. G., Brown, C. H., Werthamer-Larsson, L., Rebok, G. W., Mayer, L. S., et al. (1993). The short-term impact of two classroom-based preventive interventions on aggressive and shy behaviors and poor achievement. *Journal of Applied Developmental Psychology, 14*(317), 345. Kellam, S. G., Poduska, J. M., Ialongo, N. S., Wang, W., Toyinbo, P., Petras, H., et al. (2008). Effects of a universal classroom behavior management program in first and second grades on young adult behavioral, psychiatric, and social outcomes. *Drug and Alcohol Dependence, 95,* 5–28.
Developer	Jeanne Poduska, ScD, American Institutes for Research
Website	http://goodbehaviorgame.org/about

Table 4.3   An Evidence-Based Intervention for School-wide Intervention: School-wide Positive Behavior Interventions and Supports

Summary of the program	School-wide Positive Behavior Interventions and Supports (SWPBIS) is a prevention strategy that can be applied to support the behavior of all students. The model can be implemented for children having all levels of behavioral problems ranging from occasional noncompliance to chronic disruptive behavior (Lewis et al., 2015).
Goals	The goal of SWPBIS is to alter the school environment by developing systems and procedures that promote positive change in staff behaviors which, in turn, promote improvements in student behaviors within the classroom and in nonclassroom settings, such as the lunchroom and playground.
Target audience	Elementary, middle, and high schools.
Theory of change	SWPBIS focuses on redesigning teaching environments, not students.
Strategies offered	Implementing SWPBIS involves (a) team-based leadership; (b) data-based decision-making; (c) continuous monitoring of student behavior; (d) regular universal screening; and (e) effective ongoing professional development.
Mode of delivery	A 6–10 member team of school staff members and administrators are trained to provide leadership in implementing SWPBIS. The team attends annual training meetings, establishes an action plan, and meets at least twice a month. An external support coach provides consultation and attends a monthly meeting. The SWPBIS leadership team derives procedures and policies specific to their school. They include (1) a statement of purpose; (2) a clear definition of expected behaviors; (3) procedures for teaching expected behaviors; (4) procedures for discouraging problem behaviors; and (5) procedures for record keeping and decision-making.
Materials/ curriculum	The SWPBIS team at each school can develop their own materials for implementing the intervention at their school. Although a federally funded Technical Assistance Center does not sell materials, related commercial products can be purchased from a variety of vendors.
Abstract	A 5-year longitudinal controlled effectiveness trial of SWPBIS was conducted in 37 elementary schools. The purpose of the study was to examine the impact of training in SWPBIS on implementation fidelity as well as student suspensions, office discipline referrals, and academic achievement. Matched urban and suburban schools were randomized with 21 participating in SWPBIS and 16 as the comparison (control) condition.
Results	*Fidelity of Implementation:* A number of measures were used to evaluate fidelity. Administrators, staff, and students were interviewed. Staff also completed a survey. In addition, outside assessors evaluated the school on the key features of SWPBIS: Expectations Defined, Behavioral Expectations Taught, Systems for Rewarding Behavioral Expectations, Systems for Responding to Behavioral Violations, Monitoring and Evaluation, Management, and District-Level Support. The evaluation showed that schools trained in SWPBIS implemented the model with high fidelity. *Evidence Reported:* School-level longitudinal analyses indicated that the SWPBIS schools, compared to the comparison schools, experienced significant reductions in student suspensions and office discipline referrals.
Reference	Bradshaw, C. P., Mitchell, M. M., & Leaf, P. J. (2010). Examining the effects of school-wide positive behavioral interventions and supports on student outcomes: Results from a randomized controlled effectiveness trial in elementary schools. *Journal of Positive Behavior Interventions,12*(3), 133. doi:10.1177/1098300709334798
Website	http://www.pbis.org/

Table 4.4   An Evidence-Based Social and Emotional Learning Program: PATHS

Summary of the program	*PATHS* (Promoting Alternative THinking Strategies) is a teacher or counselor delivered social and emotional learning program that aims at facilitating the development of children's self-control, emotional awareness, and interpersonal problem-solving skills.
Goals	The main goals of the program are the promotion of social and emotional competencies, the reduction of aggression and behavior problems, and improvement of the overall classroom educational process.
Target audience	The program is targeted at preschool through grade 6 children in regular and special education classroom. *PATHS* has been used in schools serving children from diverse cultural backgrounds.
Theory of change	*PATHS* is based on the Affective-Behavioral-Cognitive-Dynamic (ABCD) Model of Development, which posits that to fully understand one's own behaviors, those of another person, or interpersonal interactions, it is necessary to take emotions, thoughts, and communication skills into account.
Strategies offered	The program teaches skills in five conceptual domains: self-control, emotional understanding, positive self-esteem, relationships, and interpersonal problem-solving. Through lessons and activities, children learn about social and emotional skills.
Mode of delivery	The program is delivered by teachers or counselors who can receive training in conducting the program through on-site or online workshops. *PATHS* is taught in classrooms using the scripted 20–30 minute lessons 2–3 times per week.
Materials/curriculum	The *PATHS* curriculum has different lessons for each grade level with content that becomes more complex as children develop. Along with the lessons, pictures, photographs, posters, and additional materials are included in the curriculum. Take-home activities also are provided.
Abstract	The Fast Track program integrated the universal *PATHS* classroom program with selective services for high-risk children. The program was conducted for three years in grades 1 through 3. Schools in Nashville, Seattle, and rural Pennsylvania were randomized to *PATHS* or to a control group. Nearly 2,000 children in 190 intervention and 180 matched comparison classrooms participated.
Results	*Fidelity of Implementation:* Teachers reported weekly to their educational consultant on the lessons that they presented. Educational consultants completed monthly observations in order to assess the quality of implementation. *Evidence Reported:* Children enrolled in *PATHS* demonstrated reduced aggression and increased prosocial behavior and improved academic engagement. School environment moderated most intervention effects resulting in stronger effects in less disadvantaged schools. Larger effects were found for students who demonstrated higher baseline aggression levels.
References	Conduct Problems Prevention Research Group. (2010). The effects of a multiyear universal social and emotional learning program: The role of student and school characteristics. *Journal of Consulting and Clinical Psychology, 78*(2), 156–168.
Developer	The program was developed by Carol Kusche, PhD
Website	http://www.pathstraining.com

Table 4.5   An Evidence-Based Intervention Focusing on Conflict Resolution: Teaching Students to be Peacemakers

Summary of the program	The Teaching Students to be Peacemakers Program teaches conflict resolution procedures and peer mediation skills.
Goal	Teach students how to manage interpersonal conflicts constructively in order to improve school safety and academic achievement. Students are also taught how to mediate other classmates' conflicts.
Target audience	Early childhood through adulthood
Theory of change	When students understand that conflict is inevitable and can be desirable because it can result in a positive outcome, they are better able to use appropriate strategies for resolving the problem.
Strategies offered	There are six step to solving the problem: 1. Describing what you want. 2. Describing how you feel. 3. Describing the reasons for your wants and feelings. 4. Reversing perspectives. 5. Inventing at least three plans to resolve the conflict. 6. Choosing one option and shaking hands.
Mode of delivery	Students receive 30 minutes of training per day from their teacher for about 20 days and then weekly training for the rest of the school year. The program can be integrated with academic subjects.
Materials/ curriculum	The program is taught with grade appropriate lessons that include case studies, role-playing activities, and simulations. The strategies can be retaught each year at a more complex and sophisticated level.
Abstract	Four 9th-grade classrooms were randomly assigned to peer mediation training or to a control condition. All classrooms studied the same World War II content. Negotiation was prompted at the end of the when student dyads who were interested in conducting different class project were paired together.
Results	*Fidelity of Implementation:* Teachers were observed when conducting the lessons by team members with additional training as needed. *Evidence Reported:* Students who were in the classroom that had peer mediation training, compared to those in the control group, were at the end of the social studies unit more knowledgeable about negotiation and peer mediation, better able to apply the strategies, and achieved higher levels of knowledge and retention of the social studies content.
Reference	Stevahn, L., Johnson, D. W., Johnson, R. T., & Schultz, R. (2002). Effects of conflict resolution training integrated into a high school social studies curriculum. *The Journal of Social Psychology, 142*(3), 305–331. doi:10.1080/00224540209603902
Developer	David W. Johnson and Roger T. Johnson
Website	www.co-operation.org

the lifelong skills that enhance personal development, support relationships, and lead to ethical work and productivity (CASEL, 2013). Educators and labor experts agree that social and emotional learning is as important as cognitive gains in supporting children's development (Durlak et al., 2011; Levin, 2012). Most of the evidence-based interventions in this book include content intended to enhance social and emotional skills.

The goals of social and emotional learning programs for children and adults are the same: recognizing social cues, managing emotions, establishing positive relationships, goal setting, problem-solving, and managing interpersonal conflict constructively (CASEL, 2013). The way that social and emotional skills are learned and expressed, however, changes as children mature. Consequently, developmentally appropriate curricula are critical for enhancing social and emotional skills.

Social and emotional interventions differ in the types of skills they emphasize and the way they present their content. *PATHS*, described in Table 4.4, focuses on understanding emotions and resolving interpersonal problems. *Teaching Students to Be Peacemakers*, described in Table 4.5, targets conflict resolution.

More than 200 school-based social and emotional learning programs have been tested in randomized controlled trials (Durlak et al., 2011). Many efficacious programs produce small-to-medium effects on the social competencies they target. Some social and emotional learning programs, like *INSIGHTS into Children's Temperament*, also enhance academic skills (O'Connor et al., 2014).

The benefits of efficacious social and emotional learning extend beyond the individuals who participate in them. Society also gains from the investment. A cost-benefit analysis of six social and emotional learning programs found that there was an $11 return for every $1 invested (Belfield et al., 2015). For example, better employment results in higher tax revenues and lower costs in public services.

MAJOR TAKEAWAYS FROM CLASSROOM MANAGEMENT RESEARCH REGARDING STUDENT DISCIPLINE

Many teachers seek ways to become more efficacious in reducing student disruptive behavior (Martin et al., 2016). Practice applications, gleaned from research, can support a comprehensive classroom management approach. Meta-analyses of school-based interventions across all age groups have identified the most effective types of programs. Universal interventions that are delivered to all children in the classroom and that focus on social and emotional content are most efficacious in reducing aggressive student behavior (Barnes et al., 2011).

The importance of reducing behavior problems among school-age children cannot be overstated. In a large study examining childhood physical aggression in three countries (the United States, Canada, and New Zealand), physically aggressive acts by boys, such as fighting with peers or bullying, predicted later delinquency (Broidy et al., 2003). That generalization, however, did not hold for girls.

Other types of disruptive behavior examined in Broidy et al. (2003) were not as ominous but still compromised children's development. Oppositional behavior, including irritability, noncompliance, and hyperactivity, did not increase the risk of later delinquency among boys or girls. Fortunately, oppositional behaviors can be reduced by effective intervention.

One way by which social and emotional learning programs reduce aggression and other disruptive behaviors is by helping children change the way that they react to ambiguously provocative situations. Instead of immediately assuming that another student or adult's action was intentionally aggressive, the student learns to pause and consider other possibilities. Learning to read others' emotions and to use problem-solving skills reduces aggressive reactions (Dymnicki et al., 2011).

Other studies offer additional takeaways for reducing student behavior problems. After conducting an extensive review of classroom management studies published during the last two decades, a panel of experts offered two practice recommendations that are based on strong evidence (Epstein et al., 2008). Not surprisingly, the recommendations are discussed over and over again in the practice literature. They include modifying the classroom to prevent problem behavior by teaching social and emotional skills.

PREVENTING STUDENT PROBLEM BEHAVIOR BY TEACHING SOCIAL AND EMOTIONAL SKILLS

The following five guidelines are derived from classroom management research conducted over the past 15 years.

Engage Students as Active Learners

One of the most powerful tools teachers have for maintaining a community of learners is keeping the students engaged in learning. Dynamic instructional modalities support students as active learners within their classroom community.

Perceiving students as active learners actually has a long history in education. Rogers (1969) advocated for student-centered learning in order to optimize student engagement. He encouraged teachers to build a learning environment that emphasizes student self-direction and discovery. For example, higher-level thinking skills are promoted when students are encouraged to take risks and solve problems individually and in small groups. Learning becomes participatory under such circumstances and academic responsibility is shared among the students and with their teacher.

When students are fully engaged, their energy is focused on the classroom activity. If their attention lapses, it may be because the lesson is too difficult, not challenging enough, or is just going on for too long. A simple solution is to change the pace of the activity.

Another strategy is to switch to a different teaching modality. For example, if the students were engaged in individual seatwork, redirect them to complete the lesson together. Of course, making format changes mid-lesson necessitates preparing alternative plans to reengage the students if the assignment falters.

Preventing problems from occurring in the first place requires student participation. As discussed in more detail in chapter 3, involve the students in articulating the classroom rules. Student input into the consequences of not following the rules they created reinforces that each child is responsible for maintaining the community of learners. In addition, students should be engaged in developing and then practicing routine classroom procedures such as lining up for dismissal or collecting lunch money.

Students have their own opinions regarding classroom discipline (Free, 2014). Consistently, they endorse the importance of establishing a classroom climate that supports their own behavioral regulation and engagement. Fair rules are important to them. Moreover, they report that students who feel bonded with their teachers exhibit less disruptive behavior.

Foster Mutual Respect

As active classroom participants, students are expected to engage respectfully with their teachers and with each other. Respective interactions are based on competent social and emotional skills. Implementing a classroom or school-wide social and emotional learning programs like the ones discussed in this book is highly recommended.

Students provide many opportunities to have their behavior redirected or corrected. Such situations can be regarded as teachable moments that have the potential to improve students' social and emotional skills.

Monitor

Classrooms are busy places. Yet, skilled teachers can monitor each individual student as well as the collective group. Arranging the classroom so that all areas are visible is essential for identifying triggers that lead to disruption. Perhaps there's a crowded area in the classroom that needs to be rearranged. Or particular students are acting in ways that annoy other students or disrupt the flow of activities. Changing seat assignments might be all that is required to restore peace in the classroom.

Close observation may also identify students who are distressed. Children who internalize their stress often provide only subtle clues to what they are experiencing (Coplan & Rudasill, 2016). For example, they may be reticent to interact with adults or peers. Encouraging a withdrawn student to discuss the events of the day privately may be a useful strategy for monitoring his or her emotional state. Some children, however, are reluctant to verbalize what is upsetting them and require a more concerted effort on the teacher's part or may need a referral to the school counselor.

Set limits

The goal of disciplining students is to teach students how to act in more socially competent ways. Two principles guide dealing effectively with disruptive student behavior. The first is that discipline is symbolic; it is not punishment (McClowry, 2014).

The second principle is "less is more (effective)." In other words, subtle types of disciplinary strategies are often all that is needed for children to correct their behavior. For example, a nonverbal signal preferably delivered discreetly to a child serves as a reminder. Sometimes all that is needed is to make eye contact or to raise an eyebrow. A subtle tap on the desk suffice.

Conferring privately with a student is very effective. They usually are amenable to teacher reasoning when they are distracting other children or engaged in minor acts of noncompliance (Romi et al., 2015). Students appreciate being spoken to without their classmates hearing the conversation. In contrast, students regard whole-class admonishments as unfair (Payne, 2015).

One of the reasons that "less is more (effective)" is because harsh punishments often lead to unengaged students. Other counterproductive strategies, according to students, include canceling recess and giving detentions (Payne, 2015). Instead students prefer an opportunity to reflect so that they can redirect their own behavior.

Some teachers permit their students to take an occasional self-imposed break if they feel the need to regain their composure or concentration. Teachers of young students often designate a place in the classroom where a student may go for a few minutes. Older students prefer a safe place outside of the classroom like the guidance counselor's office.

Teach Alternative Ways to Behave

Some students do not know what behavior is acceptable at school. They frequently exhibit disruptive or socially inept behavior because they don't know alternative ways to respond. To teach prosocial skills, clear and simple directives should be posed as statements, not questions. For example, "Michael, return to your seat" not "Michael, would you like to return to your seat?" If Michael responds positively, he should be acknowledged by specifically identifying his corrected behavior: "Michael, I like that you are sitting at your desk, ready for our next activity."

A survey of students provides insights into other effective discipline strategies (Payne, 2015). Tangible rewards, such as stickers given for good work or behavior, are regarded as beneficial by younger students, but not older ones. In general, the use of stickers should be reserved for those students who need concrete evidence that what they did was regarded positively.

All students, regardless of their age, appreciate being acknowledged for good behavior (Payne, 2015). They especially value when teachers contact their parents with positive feedback. Such communications not only reinforce the students' good behavior but also enhance teacher-student relationships.

Students who have been disciplined usually appreciate an opportunity to make amends to the classroom community. Examples of activities that contribute to the community's well-being include alphabetizing books in the classroom library or reorganizing a section of the classroom. When possible, it is best to engage the student in selecting the task, being sure that the student does not select an overly ambitious assignment.

Respond Decisively When Serious Behavior Problems Occur

Aggressive behaviors require quick and decisive teacher action (Romi et al., 2015). Lying and cheating negatively affect the classroom community. Textbox 4.2 discusses lying, cheating, and effective strategies to use when they occur.

Bullying behavior is another serious problem that requires decisive teacher action. As discussed in Textbox 4.3, bullying disrupts the classroom community and often extends outside of the classroom into the larger community. Frequently, however, teachers and other adults are unaware that bullying is occurring.

Antibullying interventions identify students who are bullies, their victims, and other peers who are bystanders. All three types of students are explained in *KiVa*, an evidence-based antibullying intervention, which is presented in Table 4.6.

Using a behavior contract can be another effective strategy for students whose repetitive disruptive behavior compromises the classroom community (McClowry, 2014). Only one discrete and tangible problem should be tackled at a time. By making the contract feasible, the student has an opportunity to exhibit positive behavior changes. A small tangible reward coupled with positive recognition reinforces the good behavior and enhances the student-teacher relationship.

A strategy of last resort is exclusion that can involve an office referral, a suspension, or expulsion from school (Romi et al., 2015). When such severe consequences have been used, excluded students report that they appreciated when their teachers calmly explain how they could have acted more appropriately. The goal is to have the student accept responsibility for the behavior rather than blaming the teacher and becoming resentful.

Given the high level of emotion surrounding an incident that leads to exclusion, however, the student may not be able to retain what was initially said (Romi et al., 2015). Another private conversation should occur after the student returns to the classroom. A positive way to end the conversation is by giving the student time to reflect on better ways to respond when a similar situation presents itself in the future.

Textbox 4.2 Problems that Disrupt Trust: When Students Lie or Cheat

Lying is a student behavior that most teachers find upsetting. Almost all children lie at one time or another. Regardless, teachers are concerned about lying because it violates their trust.

From a pragmatic viewpoint, it helps to understand that young school-age children are not intentionally lying but are trying to avoid punishment. Another reason children lie is because they are attempting to get something they want. Older school-age children, on the other hand, may recognize what they are doing was wrong but would rather risk getting caught in a lie than admit that they violated a rule.

Many of the same disciplinary strategies that have been previously discussed apply to lying as well. The situation should be handled matter-of-factly and regarded as a learning experience. The student should be asked why he or she lied. Discussing the situation can help the child understand that the statement was not truthful. At the same time, the discussion will provide an opportunity to reiterate the classroom values and behavioral expectations.

Discussing the lie with a student may not be enough to discourage such behavior in the future. To emphasize that lying is not acceptable behavior, two sets of consequences can be applied. The child can be disciplined for lying *and* for the misbehavior on which the lie was based. If a student lies frequently, then the problem should be handled with a behavior contract.

Cheating is another type of student behavior that disrupts trust. Similar to lying, cheating is dishonest. Many schools or school districts have policies that specify the consequences of cheating. If a policy on cheating has not been established at the school, a clear classroom policy should be developed.

Textbox 4.3   Problems that Disrupt Trust: Bullying

In recent years, concern about bullying has increased in the United States as well as internationally. Olweus (1993) defines bullying as aggressive behavior that occurs over time in an interpersonal relationship that is characterized by an actual or perceived imbalance of social status or physical power. Bullying occurs within a social network that involves the bully, victims, and bystanders.

Bullies typically exhibit disruptive behavior problems in addition to having internalizing symptoms, poor social skills, academic problems, and negative attitudes (Cook et al., 2010). They frequently come from homes in which parental monitoring has been lax. Longitudinal studies show that bullying is associated with criminal offences in adolescence and adulthood (Farrington et al., 2011).

Victims of bullies are typically smaller in size than the students who bully them. Both prior to the bullying and after it, the bullied victim is often a socially withdrawn child who has internalizing problems such as low self-esteem, loneliness, anxiety, and depression (Reijntjes et al., 2010).

Nishina and Bellmore (2010) observed how bullying occurs among older elementary school students. They found that most instances of bullying were witnessed by another peer. The victim was unlikely to get help from bystanders although friends are more likely to help than acquaintances. Bullying usually occurs when adults are not actively monitoring the situation. Even when adults witness bullying they seldom decisively intervene.

In general, antibullying intervention programs have modest positive effects on knowledge about and attitudes against bullying but only limited changes in reducing bullying behaviors (Merrell et al., 2008). A recent meta-analysis, however, concluded that more recent school-based antibullying interventions that were methodologically rigorous decreased bullying 20%–23% and victimization by 17%–20% (Ttofi & Farrington, 2011).

The most effective antibullying interventions include a number of components: classroom management strategies for teachers, teaching bystanders how to intervene, playground supervision, and parent meetings. A new intervention, KiVa, which is a Finnish acronym for Kiusaamist Vastaan which means "against bullying" has demonstrated efficacy. KiVa, described in Table 4.6 was developed and tested in Finland. A test of its effectiveness in schools in the United States is currently underway.

Cyberbullying is a particular type of bullying that occurs through e-mail, instant messaging, social networking sites, or by texting on cellular phones (Kowalski et al., 2008). Similar to antibullying interventions, effective strategies include helping teachers to recognize bullying and victimization. Assisting students in supporting their peers who have been victimized is also recommended.

Table 4.6   An Evidence-Based Anti-Bullying Intervention: KiVa®

Summary of the program	KiVa® is a Tier 1 and Tier 2 school-wide intervention designed to prevent bullying behavior from occurring and to intervene when cases of bullying comes to the attention of school personnel.
Goals	1. Reduce bullying behavior by enhancing the empathy, self-efficacy and antibullying attitudes of bystanders who are neither bullies nor victims. 2. Assist school personnel in preventing bullying behavior at their schools and effectively intervening in bullying cases when it occurs.
Target audience	The intervention is available in three developmentally appropriate versions: Grades 1–3, 4–6, and 7–9.
Theory of change	Bystanders that support victims reduce the status rewards of bullies and their motivation to bully.
Guiding principles	Bullies attempt to gain status and power with peers by harassing low-status children. Bullying is a group phenomenon. Bystanders can assist the bully or defend the victim and, thereby, reduce the social status of the bully and bullying behavior. School personnel can assist bystanders in defending victims when bullying is identified.
Strategies offered	Tier 1 strategies, taught in classroom lessons, aim to influence the group norms and to build capacity in all children to behave in constructive ways, to take responsibility for not encouraging bullying, and to support the victims. Tier 2 is conducted by school personnel teams. Individual and group discussions are held with the victims and bullies. In addition, prosocial peers of the victim are assisted in supporting their victimized classmate.
Mode of delivery	Classroom teachers who have received two days of training conduct 20 hours of lessons delivered in 10 sessions during the course of the school year. The students learn related content through a variety of educational materials, engage in group discussions, and role-play. In the Tier 2 intervention, a team of school personnel, who have received additional training, engage in individual and small group discussions with the victims, bullies, and high-status student bystanders.
Materials/ curriculum	Student lessons with presentation graphics with teacher guides, short films, an antibullying computer game, a website for school personnel, students, and parents, and information guides for parents. Playground personnel wear vests to remind the students that their school is a KiVa school.
Abstract	Seventy-eight schools were randomly assigned to intervention and control conditions. The participants included 8,237 youth in 429 4th–6th-grade classrooms.
Results	*Fidelity of Implementation:* Tier 2 teams met with the project team three times a year. *Evidence Reported:* Multilevel regression analyses revealed that after the intervention had beneficial effects. After participating in the intervention students in KiVa, compared to those in control schools, were less victimized and engaged in less bullying. Bystanders were also less supportive of bullies. After nine months of intervention, there was a medium effect size on peer-reported victimization and small effects on self-reports.
Reference	Kärnä, A., Voeten, M., Little, T., Poskiparta, E., Kaljonen, A., & Salmivalli, C. (2011). A large-scale evaluation of the KiVa anti-bullying program; Grades 4-6. *Child Development, 82*, 311–330. doi: 10.1111/j.1467-8624.2010.01557.x
Developer	The intervention was developed by faculty in the department of psychology and the Centre for Learning Research at the University of Turku in Finland.
Website	http://www.kivaprogram.net/

SUMMARY

In this chapter, classrooms are described as having the potential to be communities of learners. Well-functioning communities share a set of values, provide emotional and tangible support to their members, and respectfully resolve differences in opinion. Both students and teachers benefit from a well-functioning community of learners.

Over the last 15 years, research in classroom management has focused on the classroom environment, teacher actions to change students' behavior, and strategies for enhancing social and emotional skills. Effective teachers regard students as active learners and use dynamic instructional modalities to engage them in academic activities. In turn, the classroom members are expected to interact respectfully with each other.

Other behavioral expectations, developed with student input, are made explicit in a well-functioning community of learners. So are the consequences for student noncompliance or disruptive behavior. Effective teachers are consistent in how they deal with noncompliance and disruptive behavior. They exert the least amount of control necessary to deal with student behavior problems. Instead, they reason with students and assist them in enhancing their own self-regulation.

CLASS DISCUSSION

- Compare and contrast the three approaches to classroom management. Which one best matches your philosophy of classroom management?
- Explain the teacher discipline strategies you have observed teachers using. Describe the classroom discipline strategies you have observed. Which ones are effective? Have you seen any strategies that have been counterproductive?

ASSIGNMENT

Write a letter to the parents of your students explaining the classroom rules and procedures.

RECOMMENDED READINGS

Emmer, E. & Sabornie, E. J. (2015). *Handbook of Classroom Management.* New York, NY: Routledge.

Jennings, P. A. & Greenberg, M. T. (2009). The prosocial classroom: Teacher social and emotional competence in relation to student and classroom outcomes. *Review of Educational Research, 79*(1), 491–525. Retrieved from http://ezproxy.library.nyu.edu:2048/login?url=http://ezproxy.library.nyu.edu:2171/docview/214122859?accountid=12768.

Johnston, P. H. (2004). *Choice words: How our language affects children's learning.* Portland, ME: Stenhouse Publishers.

Chapter 5

Incorporating Families and Their Cultures into the Classroom Community

The students in your classroom are likely to be more racially and ethnically diverse than they were in your elementary school classroom. Multiple societal transformations including globalization, immigration, and the shifting demographics in the United States have contributed to the most diverse student population in history (Aud et al. 2010).

Over the last decade, the number of white students enrolled in public schools in the United States decreased from 28.6 million (59% of public school student population) to 25.4 million (51% of public school student population). During the same time period, Hispanic student enrollment increased from 8.6 million students (18% of public school student population) to 12.1 million students (24% of public school student population). The enrollment of black students in public schools dropped from 8.3 million (17% of public school student population) to 7.8 million (16% of public school student population) (Kena et al., 2015).

By the year 2020, 50% of the students in public schools will be students of color (Aud et al., 2012). Another indicator of the increasing diversity in schools in the United States is the dramatic increase in students whose first language is not English (Wallman, 2015). As of 2013, 22% of students speak a language other than English at home; an additional 5% of students have difficulty speaking English.

Teacher demographics, however, are much less diverse. More than 80% of teachers are white. Black and Hispanic teachers each make up an additional 7%. Only 1% of teachers are Asian and less than 1% are Pacific Islanders, American Indian/Alaska Native, or two or more races (U.S. Department of Education, 2012).

It is impossible to present an in-depth presentation of all of the social groups of students who currently attend elementary schools in the United States in one textbook. Instead, this chapter introduces culturally responsive teaching and acknowledges it as an ongoing process of incorporating the values and experiences of different cultures into the fabric of the classroom community. Culturally responsive teaching acknowledges the importance of understanding children within the context of their families.

In this chapter:

- Race, ethnicity, and the related educational repercussions in the United States are explored.
- Culture is described as a more complex concept than race.
- Information about immigrant and poor children is provided along with FYIs about English language learners (ELLs), and Hispanic, African American, Asian, Muslim children and their families.
- An example of an evidence-based intervention that is sensitive to cultural nuances of parents, *The Family Check-Up,* is presented.
- Guidelines and suggestions for incorporating multiculturism into your classroom community are offered.

WHAT IS RACE?

The genesis of racial relations in the United States can be traced to the first European explorers who encountered Native Americans soon after debarking from their ships. Fast forward hundred years and race is still a subject that permeates a great deal of attention. Race considerations are often embedded in federal and state policies and in the evaluation of their outcomes, including those related to education.

The U.S. Department of Education (2007) identifies five categories of race:

- *American Indian or Alaska Native*—original people of North and South America;
- *Asians*—any of the original peoples of the Far East, Southeast Asia, or the Indian subcontinent including Cambodia, China, India, Japan, Korea, Malaysia, Pakistan, Philippine Islands, Thailand, and Vietnam;
- *Black or African Americans*—origins in the black racial groups of Africa;
- *Native Hawaiian or Other Pacific Islander*—from Hawaii, Guam, Samoa, or other Pacific Islands; and
- *Whites*—from Europe, the Middle East, or North Africa.

Another category, *Hispanic* or *Latino* is an ethnicity, not a race. Most Hispanics are white, although some are black. The cultural origins of Latinos include Mexico, Puerto Rico, Cuba, and South or Central America.

In the United States, white, non-Hispanic people with European familial roots are currently the majority or mainstream population. The demographics of people living in the country, however, are rapidly changing. By the year 2043, although white, non-Hispanic people will still be the largest population group, no racial or ethnic group will be the majority (U.S. Census Bureau, 2010). Consequently, the term, "minority" to describe people of color in the United States soon will be outdated. Instead, as the 2010 Census reports, the United States is rapidly becoming a plurality nation with a multiplicity of ethnic groups.

Many classrooms in the United States already reflect the changing demographics of the country. An honest appraisal of teaching and learning in the United States necessitates examining how the education field is fulfilling its mandate for

Textbox 5.1   An FYI about English Language Learners

English language learners (ELL) attending public schools speak over 150 languages (Batalova & McHugh, 2010). The vast majority (73%) speak Spanish. The other languages spoken by smaller numbers of students include: 4% Chinese, 3% Vietnamese, and 2% French/Haitian Creole. The rest of the languages accounts for less than 2%. Most ELL students speak their native language at home.

Students who are ELL face a number of challenges at school as they try to learn a new language and adjust to a new culture. The dual demands can take a toll on ELL students (Curran, 2003). Many perceive themselves as less academically competent and lower in self-regulation than students who speak English fluently (LeClair et al., 2009).

A great deal of energy is required for mastering a new language simultaneously with learning academic content. Language acquisition takes time. Although conversational English occurs within a couple of years, the level of language skills necessary for classroom learning takes several years (Suárez-Orozco et al., 2011). Students who are resilient to the challenges of being an ELL often receive encouragement and tangible help from their family (Rivera & Waxman, 2011). A supportive classroom environment is another asset (LeClair et al., 2009).

providing its diverse student population with equitable educational opportunities (Textbox 5.1).

Concerns about educational inequalities have had a long history in the United States. The landmark Supreme Court case of *Brown v. Board of Education* (1954) ruled that state-sanctioned segregation was discriminatory because it denied African American students equal educational opportunities.

Funds for desegregation, however, were not made available until 11 years later when Congress passed the Elementary and Secondary Education Act (Brown-Jeffy, 2009). Integrating schools was a substantial step forward. Yet, educational inequities continue today.

ACHIEVEMENT GAPS IN EDUCATION

One of the major reasons that race and ethnicity are major concerns in the education field is due to achievement gaps. According to the National Assessment for Education Progress, an achievement gaps occurs when one group of students outperforms another group and the difference between in the groups is statistically significant (Bohrnstedt et al., 2015). A long-standing achievement gap exists between native-born white children and students who are African Americans, Native American, or Hispanic (Howard, 2010).

Disparities among racial/ethnic groups are evident in grades, standardized tests, high school graduation rates, referrals and placement in special education, numbers of suspensions, and expulsion rates. The achievement gap remains even when the students are from the same socioeconomic backgrounds. For example, African American and Latino students from affluent homes in high-quality schools still underperform when compared to white children from families with the same economic resources.

Understanding why some racial or ethnic groups have lower achievement levels requires appreciating the social, political, and economic circumstances that have produced educational inequities. Persistent achievement gaps demonstrate that racial and ethnic biases still have an impact on the way children are educated in the United States. One contributor to biases resides in the confusion between race and culture.

Sometimes used as synonyms, race and culture have very different meanings. Race is a socially constructed concept that classifies individuals based on physical characteristics such as skin color, hair texture, and eye shape. Racial categories are not biologically derived or scientifically supported (Sternberg, 2012). Although ethnic/racial classifications continue to be used to assess achievement gaps in educational outcomes, they are inadequate for understanding an individual student culture.

WHAT IS CULTURE?

Culture is a much broader concept than race, and consists of the learned and transmitted beliefs, values, and practices that shape and interpret a community's activities and interactions (Gone, 2011). Shaped by the historical, economic, ecological, and political forces that a particular group of people have experienced, culture provides a framework that helps its members interpret their past, understand their customs and rituals, and set aspirations for the future (Robles de Meléndez & Beck, 2010). Because culture is multifaceted, it is much broader than a particular race or ethnic group. Social class, family history, geographic locality, and religious affiliation are among the many factors that contribute to one's culture.

The primary purpose of a culture is to promote the adjustment, growth and development of individuals and of the societal group (Cuéllar, 2000). A culture's unwritten and codified rules reflect a shared understanding of the way that people are expected to behave. The core values and beliefs of a culture are its deep structures. They define the role and responsibilities of the individual and the family, gender norms, and how people are expected to relate to each other (Santisteban et al., 2002).

Children acquire culture through two mutually interactive systems within their developmental niche (Super & Harkness, 1986). The first is the environment—a composite of the physical and social settings in which a child interacts, the childrearing customs of the community, and the psychology of the child's caregivers which is reflective of their own culture. In multiple ways, the environment relays messages to the child regarding expectations for behavior. The second system consists of child's own contribution to the developmental niche based on his or her temperament.

Adults from different cultures perceive some behaviors as challenging and endorse others (Gartstein et al., 2010). For example, one of the distinctions between various cultures is the emphasis placed on individuality versus group harmony. In North American and many other Western cultures, adult encourage children to be assertive. Children are encouraged to assert themselves especially when they encounter a challenging situation.

Table 5.1   The Family Check-Up

Summary of the program	The Family Check-Up is a culturally relevant intervention that aims to reduce children's problem behaviors by enhancing parental involvement.
Goal	The primary goals of the Family Check-Up are to identify the family's strengths and areas of concern so that research-based interventions can be tailored to meet the family's specific needs.
	The specific intervention goals include enhancing parental monitoring of their child's safety, behavior, feelings, and experiences, and whereabouts by applying positive behavior support, setting healthy limits, and enhancing family relationships.
Target audience	Families from many cultures who have children ranging from toddlers to adolescents have been engaged in the Family Check-Up.
Theory of change	The theory of change for the Family Check-Up comes from social learning theory which asserts that noncompliant child behavior is reinforced by parental acquiescence to a child's oppositional behavior. Over time, conflict between parent and child escalates and when parents fail to monitor the child's behavior, it typically becomes more deviant.
Strategies offered	The Family Check-Up begins with a comprehensive assessment that provides parents with a realistic appraisal of their family's functioning. Feedback about the assessment findings emphasizes strengths and targets challenges in family management. Parents are then provided options for learning specific family management skills.
Mode of delivery	The intervention begins with three sessions that include an interview, a comprehensive assessment, and feedback that includes discussion about family relationships and child management skills. Families who need additional support are given individually tailored evidence-based parenting intervention.
Materials/ curriculum	A website has been developed that provides information about the intervention. Training and supervision in delivering the Family Check-Up is offered. Books and other intervention materials are available.
Abstract	Nearly 600 ethnically diverse families with middle school children were randomly assigned to the Family Check-Up condition or to a control group.
Results	*Evidence Reported:* Parents who participated in the Family Check-Up compared to those in the control group had significantly less growth in family conflict. Their children participated in less antisocial behavior and less involvement with deviant peers and alcohol use.
References	Van Ryzin, M. J., Stormshak, E. A., & Dishion, T. J. (2012). Engaging parents in the family check-up in middle school: Longitudinal effects on family conflict and problem behavior through the high school transition. *Journal of Adolescent Health, 50*(6), 627–633. doi: http://dx.doi.org/10.1016/j.jadohealth.2011.10.255
	Dishion, T. J., & Stormshak, E. A. (2007). *Intervening in children's lives: An ecological, family centered approach to mental health care.* Washington, D.C.: American Psychological Association.
Developer	The University of Oregon Child and Family Center
Website	https://fcu.cfc.uoregon.edu

In more collectivist cultures such as China, self-control is highly valued and encouraged. In fact, inhibited or shy behavior is perceived as an expression of social competence (Chen, 2010).

The contrast between individualistic and collectivist cultural perspective is also apparent in the regulation of emotions (Trommsdorff & Cole, 2011). For instance, demonstrating anger in Asian countries is particularly discouraged because it threatens interpersonal harmony. In contrast, parents in Western cultures value the expression of joy, happiness, and pride. Likewise, whereas shame is regarded negatively in Western cultures and associated with adjustment problems, shame is valued in Asian societies because it demonstrates that children are deferring to authority and understand their role within the larger community.

The distinction between the socialization goals of parents in individualistic and collectivist cultures is just one of many ways that cultures differ. Other examples include, but are not limited to, behavioral expectations for girls compared to boys and parental expressions of warmth and disciplinary strategies.

Another parenting aspect that is influenced by culture is the way that parents are engaged in their children's education. Multiple studies have shown that parental involvement at school has positive effects on children's academic achievement (Jeynes, 2012). Parental involvement is an expectation in the majority of American schools. Some cultural groups, however, are reluctant to be engaged for a variety of reasons. For example, Hispanic parents respect teachers and do not want to be perceived as interfering with their authority. (Suárez-Orozco & Suárez-Orozco, 2001). *The Family Check-Up* is an evidence-based intervention that is sensitive to cultural nuances of parents (Table 5.1).

TEACHER EXPECTATIONS

Because culture is integral to one's identity and worldview, it is easy to assume that everyone has the same cultural perspective. Unless a conscious effort is made to learn cultural differences, misunderstandings can occur regarding race, ethnicity, religion, or any other type of social grouping. If teachers do not understand their students' culture, they may inadvertently devalue, censure, or punish students for behaviors that are culturally appropriate.

Children experience cultural incongruence when behaviors that are valued or accepted at home are regarded negatively at school. In response, some students feel confused. Others feel marginalized or resentful. Unfortunately, episodes of cultural incongruence occur all too often in classrooms. Subtle behaviors can relay a teacher's low expectations for some racial/ethnic groups of students as opposed to others. In a meta-analysis, Tenebaum and Ruck (2007) found that teachers have higher expectations for white students than for African American and Hispanic children and that they provide the white children with more positive feedback.

Another study showed that differences in teacher behavior based on students' racial and cultural groups convey different expectations to students (McKown & Weinstein, 2008). Teacher expectations were higher for white and Asian students than they were for African American and Hispanic students even though all the students began the school year with the same levels of achievement. At the end of the academic year, students whose teachers had lower expectations demonstrated more of an academic gap than their peers who did not perceive teacher bias.

STEREOTYPES

A natural tension exists between recognizing a culture's traditions and respecting its members as distinct individuals. Cross-cultural comparisons emphasize differences in values and traits between cultures. Such contrasts are valuable when they lead to an appreciation of the cultural heritage and strengths of a group of people.

Still it is important to realize that cross-cultural differences are generalizations based on averages within a cultural group. They do not take into account the heterogeneity that exists among the individuals in the group. Instead, they can easily result in stereotyping, which occurs whenever attributes are used to characterize *all* individuals within a social group (Buchtel, 2014).

A common stereotype is that Asians are better at math than other racial groups. True, *on average*, Asian students perform better on standardized math tests than white or black students (Hemphill & Vanneman, 2011). However, teachers who expect all of their Asian students to excel in math will be disappointed. *Not all* Asian students are good at math.

Other stereotypes categorize various racial and ethnic groups in demeaning ways, such as being low in intelligence, lazy, or disrespectful. Negative stereotypes are detrimental and can undermine a student's self-concept. As already discussed, negative stereotypes also adversely affect the academic performance of students.

Stereotypes exist about a myriad of social groups including (but not limited to) particular races, ethnicities, religions, and socioeconomic levels. One of the most effective ways to dispel stereotypes is to learn more about the individuals from the various social groups. Two social groups, immigrant families and children of poverty, encounter many challenges that complicate their academic achievement.

Also included in this chapter are FYIs about two races (African American and Asian), and two ethnic groups (Hispanic and Muslim). At least some of the students in your future classrooms are likely to belong to one or more of these diverse groups (Textboxes 5.2–5.5).

IMMIGRANT CHILDREN

The vast majority of people who immigrate to the United States anticipate a better life for themselves and, even more so, for their children (Suárez-Orozco et al., 2008). Sometimes the primary impetus for immigration is the political circumstances in the native country that make life untenable or even life threatening. For others, the major motivation is financial because there are too few available jobs in the nativity country. Frequently, people immigrate for both reasons.

The number of immigrants in the United States has grown rapidly in recent years. Currently, almost 10% of children in schools were either born in another country or

Textbox 5.2   An FYI about Hispanics in American Elementary Schools

Children from Hispanic families are the fastest growing group in the United States. Projections by the U.S. Census Bureau (2012) suggest that by 2025, nearly one in every three children will be of Hispanic ancestry.

Several cultural values are widely acknowledged as central to the way that parents socialize their children (Halgunseth et al., 2006). Anchored in a collectivist orientation, the Hispanic culture emphasizes family unity, responsibility, and parental authority. *Familismo* refer to an individual's obligation to the family, which is exhibited in frequent contact and reciprocity among nuclear and extended family members. *Respeto* promotes harmony within interpersonal relationships both in and out of the immediate home setting. Roles are clearly defined and behavioral expectations are clear.

Another related cultural value, *educación,* is far more comprehensive than the traditional American perspective of education that is equated with academic achievement. *Educación* extends to parenting practices that instill moral character and personal responsibility in children (e.g., treating others with respect, or maintaining a proper demeanor). When Hispanic children are reprimanded, they are taught to put their heads down and remain quiet as a sign of respect (Robles de Meléndez & Beck, 2012).

Despite these cultural or family assets, poverty remains a major problem for many Hispanic families living in the United States. The consequences of living in a low-income family are reflected in the academic achievement of Hispanic children. By kindergarten, Hispanic children lag behind their more economically advantaged classmates in social-emotional and academic competence (Galindo & Fuller, 2010).

Hispanic children whose parents were born in the United States, however, have fewer academic problems because the English language is less of an issue. Their parents also have more familiarity with American institutions including the educational system so that they can better advocate for appropriate resources for their children. On the other hand, Hispanic children who are highly acculturated may be less respectful to their parents and may challenge their authority (Klugman et al., 2012).

have parents who are immigrants (Aud et al., 2012). Moving to a new country always requires a number of adjustments. Acculturation is the process of taking on the values, beliefs, and language of the host country culture (Hirai et al., 2015).

As individuals acculturate, they increasingly identify and feel a sense of belonging with the new culture. One factor that affects acculturation and the emotional well-being of immigrant adults and their children is whether the family immigrated as a whole, which seldom is the case (Suárez-Orozco et al., 2010). Instead, the vast majority of immigrant children experience at least some period of time when they are separated from one or both parents.

When reunited with their parents, the children often experience other situations that require major adjustments. Depending on the age of the child and the length of

Textbox 5.3   An FYI about African Americans in Elementary Schools

African Americans vary widely in their educational levels, financial resources, family composition, neighborhood communities, and the parenting strategies they use to socialize their children. Although African American families disproportionately experience poverty, not enough attention has been applied to the growing numbers who are middle class (Tamis-LeMonda et al., 2008).

A strength of the African American community is the broad perspective applied to the concept of "family" (Jones et al., 2007). African American children are usually part of a family system that includes their biological parents and other extended family members such as grandparents, aunts, uncles, and cousins. Fictive kin, who are close friends or neighbors, also are part of the family.

With the support of the extended family, children are socialized to respect the larger community's values. Spirituality and church involvement are also highly valued. The extended African American family is a particular asset to single mothers, especially those that are teenagers (McAdoo & Younge, 2009). Extended families often are an asset in times of adversity. Family members share material resources and provide emotional support.

Another positive quality of the African American extended family is their ability to relay cultural pride to the children while still preparing them for the possibility of racial inequities and bias (Tamis-LeMonda et al., 2008). Unfortunately, cultural biases about African American students still remain in the educational system. Black students receive a disproportionate amount of discipline at school including office referrals and suspensions (Gregory et al., 2010).

Resiliency among low-income African American children often can be attributed to the parenting they received (Gutman & McLoyd, 2000). African American parents of high-achieving, low-income children set high expectations for their children and acknowledge them when they are successful. They carefully monitor their children's homework and intervene quickly if their children have difficulties with school work. The parents are involved at their children's school and initiate communication with school personnel. The high-achieving children are also engaged in their community in extracurricular and religious activities.

Culturally responsive teachers of African American students appreciate that their black students are often more animated than other cultural groups (Gregory et al., 2010). African American students respond to teachers who demonstrate that they care by providing individual attention (Brown, 2003). The students also describe culturally sensitive teachers as acting with authority and assertiveness and being clear about behavioral expectations. Such teachers use short clear directives avoiding not ambiguous requests or questions.

separation, they may feel disconnected to their biological parents. Even if they are relieved to be reunited with their parents, they may miss the care providers who acted on behalf of their parents during the separation.

Children may encounter other challenges when reunited with their parents. Changes in the family configuration may have happened during the separation; one of the

Textbox 5.4   An FYI about Asians in American Elementary Schools

Prior to the Immigration Act of 1965, the majority of Asians in the United States were American born, highly educated, and were middle class (Okazaki & Lim, 2011). Since then, an influx of Asians has immigrated to the United States that is more diverse in their nationality, language, income, and educational levels.

Other differences are evident among the current generation of Asian children in the United States. Sixty percent speak another language at home (Aud et al., 2010).

Regardless of their own economic resources, most Asian parents believe that education is the key to social mobility and are active agents in their children's socialization (Okazaki, 2000).

Asian parents have high expectations regarding their children's academic achievement. They provide their children with extra resources, such as tutoring (Kolker, 2012). The children are expected to associate with high achievers at school and to be successful in their extracurricular activities, such as music and sports. Parents are hesitant to be involved at school, but they are highly supportive of their children's studies in the way they structure their home and time.

High parental expectations are perceived as burdensome by some Asian children. Likewise, similar to other poor immigrant children, some Asian children feel disconnected from school and acculturate into oppositional cultural groups (Okazaki & Lim, 2011).

Some teachers regard Asian children as ideal students. Others regard them as deferential and low in assertiveness. A more nuanced perspective appreciates that their modest behavior emanates from Asian cultural values that emphasize respect for others, interpersonal harmony, and an expectation for emotional regulation (Okazaki, 2000).

parents may have a new spouse or partner and there may be additional siblings or other family members. All of these changes take a toll on the children, often resulting in depression.

Twenty-five percent of immigrants are unauthorized because they are not U.S. citizens nor do they have appropriate documentation like visas. Immigrant families with members that are undocumented are the most likely to endure separations and reunifications (Su.rez-Orozco et al., 2010). Families with undocumented members endure major stressors including worries about deportation. As a result, undocumented parents often live in the shadows—fearful that their legal status will be found out.

Acculturation can have other negative consequences. An "immigrant paradox" has been found in multiple studies (García Coll & Marks, 2011). Highly acculturated children who are immigrants or have immigrant parents often demonstrate poorer academic and behavioral outcomes than their less acculturated peers.

Education and the media are primary vehicles for acculturation (Cuéllar, 2000). Because immigrant children attend school and are likely to watch more media than their parents, they often acculturate more quickly than their parents, which can create a great deal of discord within a family. Some children so closely acculturate with their host culture that they reject their birth culture to the dismay of their parents. The

Textbox 5.5   An FYI about Muslims in American Elementary Schools

The number of Muslim students attending American schools is rapidly increasing (Sirin & Fine, 2008). Yet, many people in the United States know little about them. Muslims in the United States are ethnically and racially diverse. They come from over 100 different countries including Afghanistan, Pakistan, Bangladesh, and Iraq. In contrast to other immigrant groups in the United States, however, the majority of Muslim immigrants are well educated and of high socioeconomic status.

Often mistakenly regarded as an ethnic group, Muslims are a religious group who practice Islam (Sirin & Fine, 2008). Adults who are adherent to Islam are required to follow five principles: Faith in God and the Prophet Muhammad; prayer five times a day; financially contributing to the needy; fasting during the holy month of Islam, Ramadan; and taking a pilgrimage to see the birthplace of Islam.

Observant Muslims also follow dietary restrictions, such as abstaining from pork (halal). Other practices decree the way girls and women dress and restrict how boys and girls may interact with each other. As a result, Muslim parents are likely to view coed physical education classes and other mixed sex activities as culturally inappropriate.

Many teachers are unfamiliar with the Islamic faith and do not understand its values and practices. When teachers perceive immigrant Muslim parents as having different education values from their own, they rate the children lower in academic competence and behavior (Sirin et al., 2009). In recent years, discrimination against Muslims students has increased. In response, the children struggle to develop an identity that incorporates being a Muslim and an American (Sirin & Fine, 2008). As with all children, Muslim children need to know that they are safe and valued in their classrooms and by their teachers.

alienation can be particularly poignant when an immigrant mother stays at home while the rest of the family are engaged in school and/or work.

Peers also play a role in acculturating their classmates from other countries (Chen, 2012). For example, although parents in collectivist cultures often value inhibited behavior, fellow classmates may interpret shyness as social incompetence. The children may feel pressured at school to respond in ways that are not consistent with their temperament or socialization. As a result they may develop negative self-perceptions, feel lonely, or develop anxiety or depression.

Better mental health occurs when individuals are bicultural—adopting behaviors of the new culture while still maintaining ethnic pride in their cultural roots (Romero et al., 2014). Keeping the cultural values of one's heritage group is enculturation. Strategies that support enculturation include having a social network among immigrants from the same country.

Remaining connected to family and friends is also an asset. Skype and e-mail help families sustain their emotional bonds despite living great distances from each other. Another way is by providing tangible support. Even though immigrants often have limited resources while living in the United States, many send money and goods back to relatives in their home country. When possible, visits from relatives and friends and trips back to the country of familial roots support enculturation.

Cultural adaptation occurs when acculturation and enculturation are balanced. Children who are culturally adapted are more likely to be resilient to the inherent stressors involved in being part of an immigrant family (Gonzales et al., 2009). Teachers who are culturally responsive assist children in becoming bicultural by integrating their culture into the classroom community (Rothbaum & Rusk, 2011). They also help the children understand why behavioral expectations may be different at school compared to home.

CHILDREN OF POVERTY

Another group of students at risk for academic problems are children of poverty. In fact, poverty has a profoundly deleterious impact on children's education and adjustment. Early poverty initiates a trajectory resulting in lower school readiness that is amplified when poor children attend under-resourced schools (Yeung, 2012). Moreover, poor children are two to four times more likely to attend schools with classmates whose academic achievement is also low and who exhibit high levels of behavior problems (Duncan & Magnuson, 2011).

Poverty also affects children socially. Classmates from higher-income homes are likely to regard poor children negatively (Woods et al., 2005). Both African American and white children perceive poor children as less academically competent than their more affluent peers.

Children who are poor face many hardships including food insecurity, living in high-crime neighborhoods, and receiving inadequate health care. Homeless children and those who frequently relocate are at even greater risk for academic failure than their peers who live in stable housing arrangements (Masten et al., 2012).

Twenty-one percent of children in the United States live in poor families (Humes et al., 2011). Poverty levels in the United States are calculated yearly and are based on the numbers of members in a family. For example, in 2012, the poverty level for a family of four was an income of less than $23,050 (U.S. Department of Health and Human Services, 2012).

Families who are above the poverty line have a low income may qualify for some types of government assistance such as free or reduced school meals (Tribiano, 2012). For example, the children in a family of four with an income of less than $29,965 are eligible for free lunch at school or reduced lunch fees if their income is less than $42,643. The racial/ethnic breakdown of children who are eligible for free or reduced-price lunches includes black 74%, Hispanic 77%, American Indian/Alaska Native 68%, white 29%, and Asian 34% (Aud et al., 2010).

Disparities in income are becoming more dramatic in the United States. Since 1977, the average inflation-adjusted income of the bottom 20% of the population has only slightly increased while the top 20% increased by more than a third and the top 5% rose 50% (Duncan & Murnane, 2011).

Over the last decade, the number of children living in poverty has increased by 33%. During the same period, the achievement gap between children in low- versus high-income families grew from 30% to 40% (Reardon, 2011). Currently, the achievement gap between poor and more affluent children is more than twice as large as the gap between black and white children.

The deleterious effect of poverty can be reversed. For instance, although disruptive behavior is strongly associated with chronic poverty, it lessens when family income increases (Yoshikawa et al., 2012). In addition, high-quality schools have the potential to provide stability for children of poverty and enhance their resiliency (Buckner, 2012).

INCORPORATING MULTICULTURALISM IN THE CLASSROOM

The overall goal of *Brown v. Board of Education* (1954) was educational equity for all students. The achievement of that goal has not yet been realized, but progress continues to be made. One major change is how the education field is approaching multiculturalism. Recent shifts in pedagogy emphasize that learning about cultures benefits students from all ethnic, racial, and religious groups. An openness and appreciation of different cultural values and strengths prepare children for learning and working in a pluralistic society.

Because cultures are multilayered and always evolving, becoming a culturally responsive teacher is an endless but exciting journey (Howard, 2010). Learning more about the cultures of students and their families broadens one's worldview. Fortunately, there are guidelines and suggestions that can be gleaned from research and from experienced, culturally responsive teachers.

MYTHS ASSOCIATED WITH CULTURALLY RESPONSIVE TEACHING

Prior to offering guidelines for creating a culturally responsive classroom, three myths need to be dispelled. The first is that being "colorblind" or just treating every student as an individual is all that is necessary. Such a naïve approach negates the intrinsic importance of culture (Vincent et al., 2011).

The second myth is that everything attributed to culture should be respected. There are important exceptions. Delpit (2012) emphatically asserts that behaviors that emanated from oppression should not be condoned or regarded as culturally appropriate. For example, violence against children or adults is never an acceptable practice.

The third myth comes from a recommendation that students should have teachers who are of the same race or another type of social group. Given the great diversity of students and the limited demographic variability of teachers, matching the race/ethnicity of teachers with their students is not feasible. Besides, matching the culture of students and teachers does not necessarily reduce cultural dissonance (McGrady & Reynolds, 2013).

GUIDELINES FOR CULTURALLY RESPONSIVE CLASSROOMS

Multiculturalism and academic success can be achieved simultaneously. In a study of 76 culturally diverse schools, Wilcox (2012) found that higher student achievement was related to three teacher practices: modeling, trusting, and respectful relationships. In other words, the teacher strategies that have been discussed in previous chapters provide the foundation for expanding the classroom community of learners into one that embraces multiculturalism. Here are some other guidelines and suggestions.

Guideline 1: Appreciate the Importance of Understanding Different Cultures

- Learn more about your own culture and that of others. Have multicultural experiences by having a culturally diverse set of friends and traveling to different communities and countries.
- Be open to cultural differences. Use your listening and relationship skills to view situations through the perceptions of other's cultural lens.
- Become aware of your own biases and attitudes through self-reflection. Recognize if stereotypes negatively influence your perceptions or behaviors.
- Explore the history of political, social, and economic forces that have led to educational inequities.
- Be sensitive to how students might feel when they encounter different behavioral expectations at school compared to those that are culturally supported at home.

Guideline 2: Regard The Cultural Diversity of Your Students and Their Families as an Asset

- Value the wisdom of your students' parents. Incorporate them into the classroom community by welcoming them as resources who can share their culture and its meanings with you and your students.
- Recognize barriers that inhibit parents from being involved in their children's schools. Instead, provide childcare and translators for meetings and have school documents translated into parents' languages.
- Engage parent liaisons who can connect new families to the schools. When possible match the parents with liaisons from the same cultural group.
- Strive to achieve a partnership with your school's families and the community. Partnership occurs when communication, mutual respect, and power are shared.

Guideline 3: Use a Variety of Teaching Modalities to Capitalize on Students' Cultural Backgrounds

- Hold the same high expectations for learning for all your students.
- Use familial cultural examples when teaching so that children can relate to the topic (Gay, 2010). For example, children in rural communities will relate better to math problems related to farming than to urban exemplars.
- Implement activities that encourage biculturalism. Have a map of the world and have children identify their cultural roots. Include books in your classroom library that explain different cultures. Assign older students social study projects that encourage them to learn about issues that impact the communities in which they currently live as well as their country of origin.

- Alternate individual with cooperative group assignments. Some cultural groups, like African American, Hispanic, Alaska Native, and American Indian, prefer group activities (Wilcox, 2012). Encourage students from different cultural groups to work together and learn from each other.

Guideline 4: Provide Particular Support to Students Who are Recent Immigrants and ELLs (Curran, 2003)

- Learn about the cultural background of your ELL students and those who recently immigrated to the United States.
- Follow classroom routines so that the day can be more predictable.
- Assign a "buddy" to a new ELL. Try to match the ELL student with a classmate who also knows the new student's native language.
- Keep ELL students engaged. Provide them with a desk near the front of the class.

SUMMARY

In this chapter, culturally responsive teaching is defined as an ongoing process of incorporating the values and experiences of different cultures into the fabric of the classroom community. The culture of children and their families are assets when creating a multicultural classroom community.

The shifting demographics of the United States are impetuses for incorporating more multiculturalism into the classroom community. Within a couple of decades, there will be no majority race in the country. Although white people with European ancestry will be the largest group, other racial/ethnic groups are increasing, particularly Latinos.

Another motivating factor is the academic achievement gaps existing among some racial and other social groups due to the political, social, and economic forces that have created educational inequities. Racial categories are a socially constructed categorization that often leads to stereotypes. Teachers who use a broader cultural lens appreciate how culture is related to parent socialization practices and children's behavior. Culture promotes the adjustment of individuals and ordains behavioral expectations.

Adjusting to a new culture is always complicated especially when it requires learning a new language. Children who achieve biculturalism have better academic and emotional outcomes compared to those that only relate to the native country. Biculturalism is a balance between acculturating to a new culture and enculturating, which is having pride in one's ethnic roots.

Teachers can support their students in becoming bicultural in a number of ways including learning about their own culture and being open to the culture of others. Perceiving multiculturalism as an asset for all students who live in the increasing pluralistic American society leads to other teaching strategies. Examples include regarding parents as cultural resources and embedding lessons about culture into academic subjects. Maintaining a social justice stance will also enhance the equitable learning of all students.

RELATED WEBSITES

The National Center for Education Statistics: http://nces.ed.gov/programs/coe/introduction2.
  asp.
The National Center on Immigrant Integration Policy: www.migrationpolicy.org/ellinfo.html.

CLASS DISCUSSION

Think about a holiday that your family celebrated each year. Tell your classmate/col-
leagues about it: Which holiday was it? Who attended the celebrations? What did the
adults do? What did you and the other children do? Were there any particular types of
food involved? Did your celebration reflect your ethnic or racial background?

ASSIGNMENTS

* Pick a holiday that is celebrated in a culture different from your own. Ask your
  students and their families from that culture to help you plan activities so that all of
  class can enjoy the holiday.
* Using the U.S. Census Bureau website (http://www.census.gov/schools/), prepare a
  classroom lesson on a state's demographics.
* Select developmentally appropriate children's books with characters from different
  cultures.

RECOMMENDED READINGS

Howard, T. (2010). *Why race and culture matter in school: Closing the achievement gap in
  America's classrooms.* New York: Teacher's College Press.
Robles de Meléndez, W., & Beck, V. (2012). *Teaching young children in multicultural classrooms: Issues, concepts, and strategies.* (4th ed.). Belmont, CA: Wadsworth.
Trommsdorff, G., & Cole, P. M. (2011). Emotion, self-regulation, and social behavior in cultural contexts. In X. Chen and K. H. Rubin (Eds.), *Socioemotional development in cultural
  context* (pp. 131–163). New York: The Guilford Press.

Chapter 6

Special Needs Students

All classroom communities are comprised of students with an assortment of characteristics that influence their behavior at school. This chapter focuses on a group of children who have special needs. The definition of "special needs students" varies by state. In a broad sense, special needs students have an identified disability, health, or mental health condition that requires special education services and other supports. Often, the term disability is used interchangeably with special needs although disability is a narrower classification than special needs.

A dramatic change has occurred over the last forty years in the way that children with special needs are educated (Kitmitto, 2011). Increasingly, students with disabilities are integrated into regular education classrooms. As a result, regular education teachers are teaching students with intellectual, physical, or mental conditions that differ from typically developing children.

Changes also have occurred in the roles of special education teachers. Rather than teaching small numbers of special needs students in self-contained classrooms, many special education teachers are coteaching in classrooms with regular education teachers or are providing consultation to them. Frequently, regular and special education teachers are part of a multidisciplinary team that designs, implements, and evaluates the effectiveness of individualized interventions intended to address the academic and behavioral needs of special needs students.

In this chapter, some of the multiplicity of conditions and circumstances that influence the behavior of special needs students will be presented. In addition, teacher strategies will be suggested to help special needs students and their typically developing classmates reach their potential. To be good collaborators, regular education and special education teachers need to share a common language. One of the communication challenges is the number of special education terms that referred to by acronyms. Although a thorough understanding of the terminology of special education is beyond the scope of this book, this chapter begins by answering frequently asked questions (FAQs) about the acronyms.

- What is IDEA?
- Who is served by IDEA?
- What is ADHD?

- What is an EBD?
- How does RtI apply to special needs students?
- What is an FAB?
- What is ABA?
- An example of an evidence-based intervention using a daily report card is presented.
- The chapter ends by discussing classroom management strategies that are particularly effective with special needs students.

WHAT IS IDEA?

To understand current educational policies for children with special needs, you will need to flash back 50 years. At that time, many students with disabilities were taught in separate schools or in self-contained classrooms with little contact with their typically developing peers. Today, the inclusion of special needs students in regular education classroom has become more the norm than the exception. Currently, more than 80% of special needs students spend most of their school day in regular education classrooms.

Inclusion policies can be traced to a series of federal laws now referred to as the Individuals with Disabilities Education Act (IDEA, 2004), last enacted in 2004. IDEA mandates free and appropriate public school education for **all** children and youth with disabilities who are between 3 and 21 years of age. The education of students with disabilities is required to be in the least restrictive environment (LRE).

IDEA further stipulates that students with disabilities have access to the general education curriculum in their neighborhood schools as well as support services and supplemental aids. Other components of IDEA include the provision of culturally appropriate and family-oriented services. IDEA also mandates positive behavior support (PBS) to reduce behaviors that interfere with a student's learning and the classroom environment.

In response to IDEA, models of special education services for children with disabilities exist on a continuum (Erten & Savage, 2012). Full inclusion occurs when children with disabilities are fully integrated into a regular education classroom with their typically developing peers. The next level of special education services includes an "in and out" model: students with disabilities spend some of their school time in regular education classrooms and receive pullout and resource instruction outside their classrooms.

Another model of serving children with special needs is a classroom with two teachers—one of whom is a general education teacher and the other is a special education teacher who focuses most of the time on students with disabilities. The far end of the continuum is a self-contained classroom that includes only children with disabilities.

WHO IS SERVED BY IDEA?

Services covered by IDEA are provided to approximately 6.5 million children or nearly 13% of the public school students in the United States (IDEA, 2004).

A student's placement in special education services is often due to learning problems but can be associated with other factors as well (Hibel et al., 2010). Boys are referred for special education services more often than girls, especially if they demonstrate disruptive behavior problems.

Students whose readiness for school is low or who demonstrate low task engagement in the early grades are often referred to special education. The type of school that a child attends also makes a difference. Low-achieving students who attend schools in which the majority of students have high levels of academic achievement receive more special education referrals and services. African American and Hispanic students who attend low-performing schools receive the least number of referrals.

About 37% of the students who receive services have a specific learning disability (SLD)—which is a disorder that interferes with understanding or using spoken or written language. SLDs result in an inability to adequately listen, think, speak, read, write, spell, or do mathematical calculations. Another 22% of students have speech or language impairments; 11% have health impairments such as diabetes, asthma, sickle cell anemia, or epilepsy. Intellectual disabilities, autism, emotional disturbances, and developmental delay each account for 6%–7% of the special needs students. Less than 2% of children have disabilities related to hearing or vision or have multiple disabilities.

The importance of using PBS for children with special needs cannot be overstated. A great deal of empirical support demonstrates that academic achievement is intricately linked with emotional and behavioral development and vice versa (Zeng et al., 2013). Children who have disabilities are at high risk for having inadequate social skills and behavioral problems (Reed et al., 2011).

Several interacting factors contribute to the social-emotional difficulties children with special needs often exhibit (Elksnin & Elksnin, 2004): inadequate communication skills, difficulty interpreting other's emotions, central nervous system dysfunctions, and comorbid mental health conditions such as depression. The social-emotional problems of special needs students are often related to their intellectual abilities. Students with IQs below 40 have significant deficits in learning, functional, and language skills (Alquraini & Gut, 2012).

One of the impetuses for expanding the number of inclusive classrooms was the supposition that providing special needs students with opportunities to interact with typically developing peers would enhance their social skills. A number of studies have examined the interpersonal relationships that occur in inclusive classrooms. The results, however, demonstrate that integrating special needs students into regular classrooms is challenging for the various members of the classroom community.

Although they accurately assess their own academic performance, special needs children overestimate their social competencies (Nowicki, 2003). Their teachers, however, perceive students with disabilities as low in social competence. The low level of social skills of many students who have disabilities interferes with their ability to make friends. Like their typically developing peers, having a good friend is motivating and makes school enjoyable (McCoy & Banks, 2012). Special needs students who are athletic tend to be popular (Avramidis, 2010). The majority of students with disabilities, however, have few close friends among their typically developing classmates (Reed et al., 2011). Instead, they gravitate to other students with disabilities.

Social skills interventions can help children with disabilities make friends. A meta-analysis of social skills training for students with special needs found that two-third of the children improved (Cook et al., 2008). Another study, however, found only small effects from social skill interventions (Kavale & Mostert, 2004).

Clearly, more research needs to be done to find better ways to enhance the social skills of children with disabilities. Still, the existing body of knowledge offers effective teacher strategies to enhance the social and emotional competence of special needs students. A number of interventions have focused on students with ADHD and EBD.

WHAT IS ADHD?

Attention deficit/hyperactivity disorder (ADHD) is a common childhood disorder that is estimated to affect about 5% of school-age children (APA, 2013). Boys are twice as likely as girls to be diagnosed with ADHD. The primary features of ADHD are a persistent pattern of inattention or hyperactivity-impulsivity or both, which interferes with a child's social and/or academic development. Students who have attention problems in the classroom frequently have related functional impairment such as difficulty focusing on their assignments or being disorganized. Students with hyperactivity have high levels of motor activity and are often restless. Impulsivity is related to behaviors that are impulsive or which are socially intrusive.

Another criterion for ADHD is that the symptoms have been consistent since before the child was 12 years old. ADHD is a lifelong condition with a genetic and neurological basis (Barkley, 2007). An assessment of a child for ADHD should include multiple adults who have observed the child in different settings (APA, 2013). In addition to parental reports about the child's behavior at home, it is important to get information from the child's teacher or other school personnel about school behavior.

Treatment for ADHD includes stimulant medications, behavioral interventions, or a multimodal treatment that includes both medication and a behavioral intervention. After reviewing various types of treatments, Pelham and Fabiano (2008) recommend that group behavioral interventions like those conducted in classrooms be implemented first. Medications reduce symptoms of ADHD like inattentiveness or motor activity but does not improve functional skills like finishing assignments or getting along with peers.

Conversely, group behavioral interventions are not as effective in reducing inattentiveness or motor activity (DuPaul et al., 2012). Children with ADHD whose behavioral issues are left untreated can advance from noncompliant to oppositional behaviors that are more difficult to treat (Kapalka, 2005). The same progression of behavioral problems can occur with other children who do not have ADHD. Both groups of children are identified as having an EDB.

WHAT IS AN EBD?

Another group of students who are increasingly integrated into regular classrooms are children with emotional and behavioral disorders (EBD). The term, EDB, is a broad classification that includes children with internalizing problems like anxiety or depression and those with externalizing behaviors such as aggression or oppositional defiant disorder.

Many children classified as EBD exhibit both internalizing and externalizing disorders. They often have depressed feelings or exhibit behaviors that interfere in their relationships with peers and teachers and negatively impact their academic achievement (Evans et al., 2004).

Children with EBD are often disadvantaged in multiple ways. Higher levels of behavioral problems are associated with socially and economically disadvantaged neighborhoods (Singh & Ghandour, 2012). Poor children are nearly 4 times as likely to have an EBD than children whose families have more financial resources.

Most children with EBD do not receive any treatment. The majority of children with EBDs who do get services receive intervention only at school (Forness et al., 2012). By the time children are identified as EBD at school, their problems are often serious, difficult to resolve, and multifaceted. Students with EBD often perform 1–3 grades lower than their typically developing peers (Vannest et al., 2009). Their social skills development also is delayed. They are at high risk for retention and dropping out of school.

Unless EBD students are a danger to themselves or others, they and students with ADHD benefit from inclusive environments rather than self-contained classrooms (Hieneman et al., 2005). Although teachers report difficulties in managing such students in their classrooms, evidence-based strategies are available to help them (Forness et al., 2012). Table 6.1 describes an evidence-based intervention that incorporates a daily report for children with EBD and ADHD.

HOW DOES RtI APPLY TO SPECIAL NEEDS STUDENTS?

Providing educational and related behavioral services to special need students requires a systematic approach. School districts that are successful in making their inclusive classrooms work effectively for their students with an EDB or other special needs share a number of characteristics (Huberman et al., 2012): their students have access to the core curriculum; special education and general education teachers collaborate well; professional development is ongoing; and RtI is carefully implemented. As discussed in chapter 3, the RtI framework is a systematic way to meet the varying level of instructional and behavioral needs of students (Fox et al., 2010). A functional behavior assessment (FBA) is recommended for children in Tier 3 services.

WHAT IS AN FBA?

The overall purpose of functional behavior assessment is to design, implement, and evaluate an individualized intervention that reduces a student's recalcitrant problem behaviors and replace them with more socially acceptable ones (Lane et al., 2011). The FBA is conducted by a team of school personnel that should include the student's classroom teacher(s), the child's parents, and the school counselor and/or school

Table 6.1   An Evidence-Based Intervention Incorporating a Daily Report Card

Summary of the program	The daily report card is a widely used evidence-based intervention for special education students with ADHD and other disruptive disorders (Fabiano et al., 2010). Although a variety of types of daily report cards exist, all of them apply a systematic data-driven procedure for targeting behaviors that compromise a student's functional status.
Goals	The primary goal of the daily report card is to improve a student's ability to function at school by reducing disruptive behaviors and improving socio-emotional skills.
Target audience	The daily report card is appropriate for students with attention deficit hyperactivity disorder and/or oppositional defiant disorder/conduct disorder.
Theory of change	Children with exhibit serious disruptive behaviors are compromised in their ability to function at school. By targeting observable behaviors, a comprehensive approach can be developed that includes frequent feedback with tangible rewards when behavioral goals are met.
Strategies offered	There are several steps to designing and implementing a daily report card: • Select the areas for improvement in consultation with school staff. Consider key domains to improve: peer relations, academic work, rule-following, and relationships with adults. • Determine how the goals will be defined. Target 3-8 behaviors depending on child's age and ability. • Decide on behaviors and criteria for the daily report card. Estimate how often the child is exhibiting the target behaviors. Set the criterion slightly higher. • Explain the daily report card to the child in a meeting that includes the teacher and the parent(s). • Establish a home-based reward system with the parent(s) and the child. • Monitor and modify the program by increasing the criterion when regularly met or by decreasing if not successful. • Trouble-shoot a daily report card that is not working and make it more appropriate. • Consider other treatments or behavioral components if trouble shooting is not adequate.
Mode of delivery	A daily report card is developed by a team that includes all the school personnel that work with the student and the child's parent(s). The student is also engaged in the process. When developed, the student's teachers provide frequent feedback to the child during the school day. In addition, the daily report card is sent home each day with the child. Parents provide home-based privileges on days when the student has been successful in meeting the targeted goals.
Materials/ curriculum	Detailed guidelines for designing and implementing the daily report card are enumerated in a 10-page worksheet that is available from the website listed at the end of this description.
Abstract	The purpose of this study was to examine whether a daily report card would improve the behavior and academic achievement of students with attention deficit with hyperactivity disorder and oppositional defiant disorder/conduct disorder. Sixty-three elementary grade school students with Individualized Education Programs were randomly assigned to an intervention using the daily report card or to a business as usual comparison group. Approximately half of the children in both groups were receiving medication for emotional and behavioral problems.

(Continued...)

Results	*Fidelity of Implementation:* Teachers completed 79% of the daily report cards and participated in 94% of the monthly consultation meetings. Parents returned 64% of the daily report cards with their signature and appropriately rewarded the children 56% of the time.
	Evidence Reported: After a year of intervention, students in the daily report card group, compared to those in the business as usual group, demonstrated better classroom functioning, higher individualized education plan goal attainment, improvements in academic productivity (i.e., work completions) and less disruptive behavior (average effect size = 0.35). There were, however, no statistically significant improvements in academic achievement.
References	Fabiano, G. A., Vujnovic, R. K., Pelham, W. E., Waschbusch, D. A., Massetti, G. M., Pariseau, M. E., . . . Volker, M. (2010). Enhancing the effectiveness of special education programming for children with attention deficit hyperactivity disorder using a daily report card. *School Psychology Review, 39*(2), 219-239.
Website	http://casgroup.fiu.edu/pages/docs/1401/1367959499_How_To_Establish_a_School_DRC.pdf

psychologist. Representatives from community agencies to whom the child might be referred may also be part of the team.

The first goal of the team is to identify the problem behaviors and target a major one (Ducharme & Shecter, 2011). At least one of the team members observes the behavior to ascertain what events predict occurrence or nonoccurrence of those behaviors and how the behaviors are maintained over time. For example, is the issue attentional (off-task behaviors), compliance with teacher directivesm, social skills with classmates, or communication? Then the team attempts to determine what the goal of the targeted behavior is for the child? For example, does it serve as an escape?

In more technical terms, the team identifies the antecedent and consequent conditions that maintain the problem behavior (Ducharme & Shecter, 2011). Then they try to identify the reinforcers for the behavior. After completing their assessment, team members will recommend how to modify the environment so that the child can use a more socially appropriate way to satisfy the identified problem behavior. For example, they may suggest ways that the student can get attention in a more positive way or how the child could communicate when a break is needed.

The results of the FBA are then compiled into a behavior intervention plan (BIP) in which short-term goals are identified and dates to evaluate progress are specified. The BIP becomes part of the student's individualized educational plan (IEP) and is revised as needed. The IEP will also list any accommodations that need to be made for the child in order for the BIP to be implemented (IDEA, 2004).

The effectiveness of a well-developed FBA to resolve the behavior problems of individual children has been documented many times—particularly for special education students (Dunlap et al., 2010). When effectively applied, FBA has moderate effect sizes in reducing problem behavior and increasing social skills (Goh & Bambara, 2012). Team interventions that engage parents increase the effectiveness of the planned intervention.

WHAT IS ABA?

Applied behavior analysis (ABA) is a highly systemic method of designing and conducting an FBA (Cooper et al., 2007). A number of methodologies exist for conducting an ABA; each has their own variations. The following section provides a general overview.

The ABA methodology is based on Skinner's (1938) operant conditioning concepts. As Cooper et al. (2007) explain, a central premise of an ABA is that the social and physical environment teaches and maintains both desirable and undesirable behavior through positive and negative reinforcements. As a result, behaviors can be reinforced without an individual's awareness.

All behavior functions as a way to seek or avoid attention, tasks, activities, tangibles, or sensory experiences (Lane et al., 2011). Positive reinforcement occurs when a behavior is followed by a stimulus that increases the likelihood that it will occur again. For example, attention, whether positive or negative, is a positive reinforcement.

Negative reinforcement, on the other hand, occurs when the stimulus results in an escape or avoidance of an aversive situation. From the child's perspective, negative reinforcement is welcomed because it terminates something unpleasant and it should not be confused with punishment.

The first step of the ABA is to identify the function of a particular behavior (Lane et al., 2011). The same disruptive behavior, such as interrupting math class with random comments, may have different functions for two children. For one child, it may be to avoid completing a math assignment that is too difficult. Another student's disruptive behavior, however, may be because the content is too easy and, therefore, perceived as boring.

As a result of their disruptions during math, both children are likely to get additional teacher attention that serves as a positive reinforcement (even if the teacher scolds the child) and a negative reinforcement if the student successfully avoids completing the assignment. Both the reinforcements increase the likelihood that the behavior will occur again. Note that neither of the reinforcements, however, deals with the underlying function of the disruptive behavior. Without that information, it is unlikely that the disruptive behavior can be replaced with a more positive one.

Standardized tools are available to help identify the relevant ABCs: A—the antecedent (the stimulus that prompts a behavior), B—the targeted behavior, and C—the consequences (Lane et al., 2011). Then an experimental design is used to systematically manipulate the various conditions with the goal of achieving reductions in the antecedents that prompt the behavior, increasing the rates of reinforcement for the replacement behavior, and/or extinction of the problem behavior.

WHAT CLASSROOM MANAGEMENT STRATEGIES
WORK FOR SPECIAL NEEDS STUDENTS?

In general, the classroom management strategies discussed in this book are applicable to both inclusive and self-contained classrooms. Regardless of the type of classroom, additional considerations are relevant for students with special needs. The following is a list of evidence-based strategies that support the emotional and learning needs of special needs students. Many also work for typically developing students.

You Matter!

- The classroom community is broadened in many ways when it includes children with special needs. Children are very perceptive. Your attitude toward the various students in the classroom will influence how they respond to each other.
- By demonstrating your own social competency skills—by being a good listener and problem-solver you teach your students important life lessons on how to deal with diversity.
- Carefully observe your students, especially for changes in behavior. Problems at home are likely to spill over into the classroom. Students who demonstrate disruptive behavior may be looking for your support. Consider, also, that a student's nonengagement may be due to depression or anxiety.
- Be flexible. Although there have been dramatic changes in the way that children with special needs are currently taught, many more are likely to occur. Your attitude toward the current system and your willingness to adapt to the changes that are likely to occur will influence not only your classroom, but also the other teachers at your school as well.

Apply PBS Strategies

- Positive behavior support is effective for all students, especially for children with special needs (Bambara et al., 2012). Minimize your use of punishments. Although they may initially stop a disruptive behavior, they quickly lose their effectiveness (Ducharme & Shecter, 2011). In addition, realize that many children cannot generalize beyond the immediate situation for which they were disciplined.
- When attempting to change a student's negative behavior, teach a more socially acceptable replacement behavior (Ducharme & Shecter, 2011). Some children do not know what behavior is expected. Teach them by providing behavior-specific praise that explicitly states the behavior you are praising.
- When attempting to understand why a student is exhibiting a disruptive or socially unacceptable behavior, observe the circumstances in which it occurs. Consider whether the behavior is related to an academic content, time of day, teacher-student interaction, or peer relationships.
- As derived from ABA (Cooper et al., 2007), select consequences that you will intentionally apply when students exhibit emotional or disruptive behaviors: positive reinforcement (praise, tangible rewards), negative reinforcement (removal of something that the student sees as negative like a homework assignment), response cost or extinction (time-out removal or the loss of privileges), or classic punishment (extra work such as cleaning the classroom or having an extra assignment).

Adapt Instructional Strategies

- Like their typically developing classmates, special needs children, particularly those who are ADHD or who have an EBD, benefit from a classroom environment that is structured and organized.
- Children cannot be on task and noncompliant (Ducharme & Shecter, 2011). Keep all of your students engaged by adapting your curriculum materials and instructional techniques to meet their particular learning needs and abilities.
- Provide yourself with adequate time to be creative with your lesson plans. Have differential instructional modalities prepared. Use appropriate assistive technology and provide students with accommodations when needed (Erten & Savage, 2012).
- Plan small group cooperative learning activities that include students with mixed abilities (Novak & Bartelheim, 2012).

Be a Good Member of the Team

- Complex student behavioral problems require a concerted team approach. A well-crafted and implemented FBA for a student takes time, expertise, effective collaboration with the child's family and other school personnel, and technical assistance for data collection and for reinforcing replacement behaviors (Chitiyo & Wheeler, 2009).
- Typically developing students become more empathic toward their classmates with disabilities when their teachers provide developmentally appropriate information about the students and when they engage in planned group activities (Novak & Bartelheim, 2012).

Above all, keep in mind that special needs students are first and foremost children. Like their typically developing peers, they are trying to make sense of the world and to identify their place in it. Solomon (2012) interviewed more than 300 parents whose children had disabilities including deafness, dwarfism, Down syndrome, autism, and severe multiple disabilities. He concluded that children with special needs must transverse dual worlds in order to accept their own, often very unique, identity.

Like all children, those with special needs live in a vertical world in which the culture of their family and community is transmitted to them (Solomon, 2012). They also occupy a horizontal world populated only by others similar to them. Parents and teachers cannot journey with children into the horizontal world but can provide acceptance, compassion, and love. Certainly, children with special needs not only require opportunities to interact with their typically developing peers, but they also need to have friends who share similar challenges and hopes.

SUMMARY

This chapter addresses classroom management applied to special needs students. The content is presented by explaining many of the acronyms that are used in special education. The Individuals with Disabilities Act is credited with many of the current inclusive classroom policies. The greatest number of students who receive special education services has learning disabilities. Others have health conditions, language impairments, emotional problems, and developmental delays.

Positive behavior support is mandated for the majority of children with special needs who have social or behavioral issues. More research, however, is needed to identify the best strategies that support the social-emotional development of special needs students. Still, a number of strategies have shown effectiveness especially for students with attention deficit with hyperactivity disorder and EBDs. Group classroom interventions are the most effective way to strengthen the functional skills of children with ADHD and are recommended before medication is prescribed.

The response to intervention framework provides a systematic way to match the level of behavioral interventions with the needs of children. Because children with EDB have multifaceted and serious behavioral and academic problems, they need intensive intervention. A functional behavioral assessment can assist teachers and other school personnel in developing and implementing individualized behavioral intervention.

Many of the previously presented classroom management strategies from this book apply to inclusive and special education classrooms. Teachers are encouraged to create a classroom community that supports the emotional and learning needs of their students with special needs as well as their typically developing peers. Collaboration with family and other school personnel is critical to achieving this goal. Above all, it is important to regard special needs students as children who seek to be accepted and loved just like their typically developing peers.

RELATED WEBSITE

http://www.nrcld.org/

CLASS DISCUSSION

- Form teams and role-play the development of a daily report card. Take turns enacting different roles: the targeted fourth-grade student, his or her parents, a teacher, and the school psychologist.
- Develop a plan on how you would pair a student with a specific disability with a typically developing classmate in a classroom activity.

RECOMMENDED READINGS

Ducharme, J. M., & Shecter, C. (2011). Bridging the gap between clinical and classroom intervention: Keystone approaches for students with challenging behavior. *School Psychology Review*, 40(2), 257–274.

Lane, K. L., Menzies, H. M., Bruhn, A. L., & Crnobori, M. (2011). Functional Assessment-Based Interventions (Chapter 7, pp. 156–179). In *Managing Challenging Behaviors in Schools: Research-Based Strategies That Work*. New York: The Guilford Press.

Volpe, R., & Fabiano, G.A. (2013). *Daily Behavior Report Cards: An Evidence-Based System of Assessment and Intervention*. New York: The Guilford Press.

Conclusion

A Not-So-Final Ending

This book ends much the same way that it began by acknowledging that the education field is undergoing exciting but challenging times. Incorporating evidence-based practices into schools holds a great deal of potential for enhancing the education and social and emotional development of students. By its very nature, science is never static but always changing.

Right now, practitioner/scientists are hard at work developing, testing, and refining evidence-based practices that you will implement in your classroom. I hope this book has prepared you for evaluating the materials you use.

Moreover, I hope that the book's content has excited you and enhanced your classroom management skills. After all, as this book has emphasized, what happens in your classroom during an academic year does not end when summer begins. Instead you continue to be an important part of your student's development long after the last day of the school year. Never underestimate how much you matter in your students' lives!

Appendix A

Welcome to Education Science City

"Educational Science City" is a fast growing community. The city planners, architects, and construction crews are working diligently because a massive amount of building and reconstruction is under way. The city has a number of neighborhoods, each of which is an education subspecialty such as literacy, numeracy, and classroom management. Work on the various neighborhoods in Education Science City is occurring simultaneously and informs the others.

Education Science City already has a number of previously built structures. Many more are needed and some of the old buildings require alterations or additions. Regardless, standard tools of the trade are employed. They include inspecting the existing foundations, engaging the community, and accessing new infrastructures.

Tools of the Trade: Building on the Existing Foundation. The first step in expanding Education Science City is to inspect the existing foundations by conducting a literature review that will explicate what is already known about a specific topic, and equally important, what is unknown. One of the challenges of conducting a literature review is shared by the construction teams of all the subspecialties: it can be difficult to shift through the literature and discriminate between conclusions based on scientific evidence and those that are derived from tradition.

A literature review compares and contrasts the findings of empirically based research studies—those that are based on data. When completed, the literature review is a synthesis that summarizes and integrates the findings of multiple studies on a topic. A completed literature review will also identify the strengths and limitations of the existing studies.

No doubt, after finishing a literature review, the conclusion will be that the amount of evidence to support educational practices is all too limited. A critique of the literature will also show that some of the previous studies had serious design flaws.

Currently, the field of education has a dilemma when evaluating its state of the science, especially in regard to the experiments that have been previously conducted. If the bar for scientific rigor is set very high, too few studies qualify as scientifically rigorous. The other choice is to broaden the criteria for evaluation and to include studies whose methodology is compromised but which are explicit about their limitations (Slavin, 2008).

One type of literature review that is gaining popularity in education is a meta-analysis in which the results from multiple studies are compared statistically (Stanovich & Stanovich, 2003). A meta-analysis is a statistical technique that compares results across related studies to produce a more definitive estimate of an effect size. For example, a school district might be interested in selecting one of several intervention programs intended to foster students' social skills. More than likely the studies that tested the programs used a variety of tools to measure changes in the social competencies of the children.

Effect sizes standardize the various test results across a number of studies so that they can be compared. Although there are several ways to calculate and report effect sizes, two types are the most frequently used (Dong et al., 2008). A Cohen's *d* is calculated when there is one continuous dependent variable (such as attentional problems) and one dichotomous independent variable (i.e., experimental or control group). The most frequently used interpretation of effect sizes are: 0.20 is small, 0.50 is medium, and 0.80 is large (Cohen, 1988). Educational and behavioral interventions are regarded as efficacious if their effect size is at least 0.25 (Dong et al., 2008).

If both the dependent and independent variables are dichotomous (e.g., improved vs. no improvement and intervention vs. control group) an odds ratio or risk ratio is used. The odds ratio is expressed by saying that one group was X times more likely to improve than the other. For example, an experiment testing whether a professional development program was effective in enhancing classroom management might use an odds ratio to describe its findings. The result might be stated as, "Following the intervention, teachers in the professional development group were 6.5 times more likely to feel efficacious in classroom management than those in the control group."

Tools of the Trade: Engaging the Community. In addition to inspecting the existing foundations, another tool, engaging the community, should be used to expand Education Science City. The community includes stakeholders such as students, parents, educators, researchers, government agencies, and social policy experts. Just as an architect would be wise to consult with the various stakeholders when designing buildings for a city, a wise developer of teaching practices engages the community in multiple ways.

Dialogue with teachers, school administrators, and consumers helps to assure that the practices being designed will be relevant to those who will use them. When planning curriculum and intervention programs, consulting with teachers is critical. They play a vital role in evaluating whether the intended practices are feasible in the real world practice settings of classrooms.

Planning a classroom management program will not occur all at once but involves many stages and multiple iterations with suggestions from teachers, school administrators, and depending on the type of intervention, perhaps, parents and even the students themselves. Developers begin by asking, "Who is this intervention for?" Then a number of creative activities begin that should involve the relevant stakeholders.

Attractive program materials need to be designed that match the learning needs of the intended participants. The materials should be examined to assure that they are developmentally appropriate for the intended recipients.

Likewise, readability should be assessed. The intervention, when completed, will be manualized so that the intervention will be standardized and consistent with the way that the developer(s) intended. To promote implementation fidelity, developers of interventions often provide training and supervision to those who implement the intervention.

Building Education Science City also requires engaging other members of the community who will critique the research design. A number of mechanisms exist that are intended to help researchers improve their research designs. Researchers at all levels of preparation need to be open to criticism, assessment, and frequent revisions. For example, university faculty members contribute toward the development of a student's research plan by overseeing student theses and doctoral dissertations.

Likewise, research proposals by faculty members who seek funding for their research ideas are critiqued by university committees, professional organizations, foundations, and/or federal agencies. Panels of experts review the proposal, often providing constructive feedback for improving the research design.

After a study is conducted, the findings will be evaluated in other forums. Professional organizations consisting of panels of experts select the studies that are presented at their conferences. Manuscripts submitted to peer-reviewed journals are critiqued by knowledgeable colleagues who can accept the manuscript for publication, offer suggestions for revisions, or reject it. Funding, needed to develop and test the efficacy of interventions, comes from universities, professional associations, foundations, and a number of federal agencies.

Tools of the Trade: Accessing New Infrastructures. Another related tool, accessing new infrastructures, will further accelerate the growth of Education Science City. A number of recently developed infrastructures are intended to quickly advance the science of education. The National Research Council (2005) has proposed several ways to advance the production of evidence-based practices:

- Promote rigor in research studies to strengthen and broaden the knowledge base;
- Enhance the professional development of researchers engaged in conducting their own studies and in providing peer review for others; and
- Enhance the partnerships between researchers and school personnel.

To meet the new demands for a larger cadre of researchers who conduct randomized experiments in schools, additional training monies have been made available for graduate students and postdoctorates, as well as faculty. With more well-qualified educators who are well prepared to use the tools of the trade, Education Science City is showing rapid growth!

Checklist for Preparing and Maintaining Your Classroom

BEFORE THE SCHOOL YEAR BEGINS

Prepare a safe and warm environment—

- Assure that procedures are in place so that only people who are safe enter the school and your classroom.
- Prepare classroom and school displays that welcome the students to the new school year.
- Prepare information about the school and your classroom for your students' parents. Explain your visiting policies to the parents.

Strategize on how to arrange the physical layout of your classroom space—

- Arrange the furniture so that there is an adequate space for the students to move with ease into the various locations like the library area, restroom, or choice centers.
- Arrange the classroom so that student traffic does not go through designated work areas. Think about using *sign posts* (such as arrows) to communicate directions.
- Avoid placing too many learning materials near the exit, the sink, or the meeting areas.
- Place your reading area away from the more interactive learning centers.
- Plan designated areas for students who desire a quite environment and for those who prefer more social interactions.
- Plan to have students do messy work where the "mess" will not interfere with other student activities.
- Be sure that you are able to monitor your students from everywhere in the room and that your students can see you.
- Plan adequate space and storage for students' personal belongings and for receiving notes and materials from their parents:
  - Clearly label all materials and their storage compartments. Color code when possible and use child-friendly language, pictures, and/or illustrations.

- ◦ Cubbies or mailboxes are recommended for younger students and folders are suggested for older students.
- ◦ Consider using color-coded storage areas. For example, things in *red* compartments stay at school; things in *blue* compartments go home.

Plan the seating arrangement of your students—

- • Assure that there is enough "elbow room" for students when engaged in table work or for class meetings.
- • Alternate boys and girls in your arrangements.
- • Place students with disruptive behavior near the front of the room.
- • Use rows for times when you want student attention to be directed at you.
- • Prepare an alternative room arrangement for times when you would like students to work together.
- • Plan classroom procedures and routines:
  - ◦ Think about how the children will move furniture (like their chairs) for the various class functions.
  - ◦ Decide how often and under what circumstances you will allow students to enter and exit the classroom.
  - ◦ Plan procedures for noninstructional activities such as collecting lunch money, taking attendance, or collecting permission slips. Establish routines so that the students handle such matters independently and unobtrusively.

During the early weeks of the school year

- • Practice class and school procedures with the students.
- • Conduct class meetings with the students to establish class rules or procedures.
- • Provide positive and clear corrective feedback regarding students' performance in carrying out organizational activities.
- • Replace the displays that you made for the beginning of the school year with student work.

Throughout the school year

- • Monitor the behavior of the students. Provide positive feedback when their behavior is appropriate.
- • Prepare instructional materials and supplies prior to the students' arrival each day.
- • Label and store materials that are intended for your students to use at their eye level.
- • Place materials that you *do not* want the children to use in areas that are not accessible to them.
- • Avoid clutter. A clean and organized room sets a good example for your students regarding their own desks and school work.
- • Post a developmentally appropriate daily and weekly schedule so that the students know what to expect.
- • Observe how students are using the various portions of your classroom. If a change in the room arrangement needs to be made, discuss the reason with the students.

Involve the students in planning the changes and in identifying potential stumbling blocks.
- Be consistent in the strategies you and other adults in the classroom use in response to student noncompliance or disruptive behavior.

REPRINTED FROM

McClowry, S. G. (2014). *Temperament-based elementary classroom management.* Lanham, MD: Rowman & Littlefield.

References

Ainsworth, M. S. (1989). Attachments beyond infancy. *American Psychologist, 44*(4), 709–716. doi:10.1037//0003-066x.44.4.709

Alquraini, T., & Gut, D. (2012). Critical components of successful inclusion of students with severe disabilities: Literature review. *International Journal of Special Education, 27*, 42–59.

American Psychiatric Association [APA]. (2013). *Diagnostic and statistical manual of mental disorders* (5th ed.). Arlington, VA: American Psychiatric Association.

Arbeau, K. A., Coplan, R. J., & Weeks, M. (2010). Shyness, teacher-child relationships, and socio-emotional adjustment in grade 1. *International Journal of Behavioral Development, 34*(3), 259–269. doi:10.1177/0165025409350959.

Aud, S., Fox, M., & KewalRamani, A. (2010). *Status and Trends in the Education of Racial and Ethnic Groups* (NCES 2010-015). U.S. Department of Education, National Center for Education Statistics. Washington, DC: U.S. Government Printing Office.

Aud, S., Hussar, W., Johnson, F., Kena, G., Roth, E., Manning, E.,… Notter, L. U.S. Department of Education, National Center for Education Statistics. (2012). *The condition of education* (NCES 2012045). Retrieved from website: http://nces.ed.gov/pubsearch/pubsinfo.asp?pubid=2012045.

Avramidis, E. (2010) Social relationships of pupils with special educational needs in the mainstream primary class: peer group membership and peer-assessed social behavior. *European Journal of Special Needs Education, 25*(4), 413–429. doi: 10.1080/08856257.2010.513550.

Baker, J. A., Clark, T. P., Maier, K. S., & Viger, S. (2008). The differential influence of instructional context on the academic engagement of students with behavior problems. *Teaching and Teacher Education, 24*(7), 1876–1883. doi: 10.1016/j.tate.2008.02.019

Bambara, L. M., Goh, A., Kern, & Caskie, G. (2012). Perceived barriers and enablers to implementing individualized positive behavior interventions and supports in school settings. *Journal of Positive Behavior Interventions, 14*(4), 228. doi: 10.1177/1098300712437219.

Barkley, Russell A. (2007). School interventions for attention deficit hyperactivity disorder: Where to from here? *School Psychology Review, 36*(2), 279–286.

Barnes, T. N., Smith, S. W., & Miller, M. D. (2014). School-based cognitive-behavioral interventions in the treatment of aggression in the United States: A meta-analysis. *Aggression and Violent Behavior, 19*(4), 311–321. doi:10.1016/j.avb.2014.04.013.

Batalova, J., & McHugh, M. Nation Center on Immigration Integration Policy, Migration Policy Institute. (2010). *Top languages spoken by English language learners nationally and by state.* Retrieved from website: http://www.migrationinformation.org/ellinfo/Fact-Sheet_ELL3.pdf.

Bear, G. G. (2015). Preventive and classroom-based strategies. In E. Emmer & E. J. Sabornie (Eds.). *Handbook of Classroom Management* (2nd Ed., pp.15–38). New York, NY: Routledge.

Belfield, C, Bowden, B., Klapp, A., Levin, H., Shand, R., & Zander, S. (2015). *The economic value of social and emotional learning.* Report from the Center for Benefit-Cost Studies in Education: Columbia University.

Berry, D., & O'Connor, E. (2010). Behavioral risk, teacher–child relationships, and social skill development across middle childhood: A child-by-environment analysis of change. *Journal of Applied Developmental Psychology, 31*(1), 1–14. doi:10.1016/j.appdev.2009.05.001.

Bohrnstedt, G., Kitmitto, S., Ogut, B., Sherman, D., and Chan, D. (2015). School Composition and the Black–White Achievement Gap (NCES 2015-018). U.S. Department of Education, Washington, DC: National Center for Education Statistics. Retrieved September 24, 2015 from http://nces.ed.gov/pubsearch.

Bowlby, J. (1969). *Attachment and loss.* New York: Basic Books.

Boyer, E. L. (1991). *Ready to learn: A mandate for the nation.* Princeton, NJ: Carnegie Foundation for the Advancement of Teaching.

Braden, J. P., & Shernoff, E. S. (2008). Why the need for evidence-based interventions? In R. J. Morris, & N. Mather (Eds.), *Evidence-based interventions for students with learning and behavioral challenges* (pp. 9–30). New York, NY: Routledge.

Bradshaw, C. P., Schaeffer, C. M., Petras, H., & Ialongo, N. (2010). Predicting negative life outcomes from early aggressive-disruptive behavior trajectories: Gender differences in maladaptation across life domains. *Journal of Youth and Adolescence, 39*(8), 953–966. doi: 10.1007/s10964-009-9442-8.

Broidy, L. M., Nagin, D. S., Tremblay, R. E., Bates, J. E., Brame, B., Dodge, K. A., . . . Vitaro, F. (2003). Developmental trajectories of childhood disruptive behaviors and adolescent delinquency: A six-site, cross-national study. *Developmental Psychology, 39*(2), 222–245. doi: 10.1037//0012-1649.39.2.222.

Bronfenbrenner, U., & Morris, P. A. (1998). The ecology of developmental processes. In R. M. Lerner & W. Damon (Eds.), *Handbook of child psychology: Vol 1. Theoretical models of human development* (5th ed., pp. 993–1028). New York: Wiley.

Brophy, J. (2006). History of research on classroom management. In C. Evertson & C. Weinstein (Eds.), *Handbook of classroom management: Research, practice, & contemporary issues* (pp.17–43). New York, NY: Simon & Schuster Macmillan.

Brophy, J., Rohrkemper, M., Rashid, H., & Goldberger, M. (1983). Relationships between teachers' presentations of classroom tasks and students' engagement in those tasks. *Journal of Educational Psychology, 75*(4), 544–552. doi: 10.1037/0022-0663.75.4.544.

Brown v. Board of Education, 347 U.S. 483 (1954).

Brown, D. F. (2003). Urban teachers' use of culturally responsive management strategies. *Theory Into Practice, 42*(4), 277–282. doi:10.1207/s15430421tip4204_3.

Brown-Jeffy, S. L. (2009). Brown v. Board of Education, Topeka, Kansas (and Brown II). In K. Lomotey (Ed.), *Encyclopedia of African American education* (pp.116–119). Thousand Oaks, CA: Sage.

Buchtel, E. E. (2014). Cultural sensitivity or cultural stereotyping? Positive and negative effects of a cultural psychology class. *International Journal of Intercultural Relations, 39*, 40–52.

Buckner, J. C. (2012). Education research on homeless and housed children living in poverty: Comments on Masten, Fantuzzo, Herbers, and Voight. *Educational Researcher, 41*(9), 403–407. doi:10.3102/0013189X12466588.

Cameron, C. E., Connor, C. M., Morrison, F. J., & Jewkes, A. M. (2008). Effects of classroom organization on letter-word reading in first grade. *Journal of School Psychology, 46*(2), 173–192. doi: 10.1016/j.jsp.2004.12.002.

Collaborative for Academic, Social, and Emotional Learning (CASEL). (2012). *2013 CASEL guide: Effective social and emotional learning programs (preschool and elementary school edition).* Chicago, IL. Retrieved January 20, 2016, from http://static1.squarespace.com/static/513f79f9e4b05ce7b70e9673/t/526a220de4b00a92c90436ba/1382687245993/2013-casel-guide.pdf.

Chen, X. (2010). Socioemotional development in Chinese children. In M. H. Bond (Ed.), *Handbook of Chinese Psychology* (pp. 37–52). Oxford, UK: Oxford University Press.

Chen, X. (2012), Culture, peer interaction, and socioemotional development. *Child Development Perspectives, 6*, 27–34. doi:10.1111/j.1750-8606.2011.00187.x.

Chitiyo, M., & Wheeler, J. J. (2009). Challenges faced by school teachers in implementing positive behavior support in their school systems. *Remedial and Special Education, 30*(1), 58–63. doi: 10.1177/0741932508315049.

Codding, R. S., & Smyth, C. A. (2008). Using performance feedback to decrease classroom transition time and examine collateral effects on academic engagement. *Journal of Educational & Psychological Consultation, 18*(4), 325–345. doi: 10.1080/10474410802463312

Collins, B. S., O'Connor, E. E., & Supplee, L. (in press). Behavior problems in elementary school among low-income males. *Journal of Educational Research.*

Conners, C. K. (2008). *Conners 3.* North Tonawanda, NY: Multi Health Systems.

Cook, C. R., Gresham, F. M., Kern, L., Barreras, R. B., Thornton, S., & Crews, S. D. (2008). Social skills training for secondary students with emotional and/or behavioral disorders: A review and analysis of the meta-analytic literature. *Journal of Emotional and Behavioral Disorders, 16*(3), 131–144.

Cook, C. R., Williams, K. R., Guerra, N. G., Kim, T. E., & Sadek, S. (2010). Predictors of bullying and victimization in childhood and adolescence: A meta-analytic investigation. *School Psychology Quarterly, 25*(2), 65–83. doi:10.1037/a0020149.

Cooper, J. O., Heron, T. E., & Heward, W. L. (2007). *Applied Behavior Analysis* (2nd Ed.). Upper Saddle River, N. J.: Pearson Prentice Hall.

Coplan, R. J. & Rudasill, K. M. (2016). *Quiet at school: An educator's guide to shy children.* New York, NY: Teachers College Press.

Cornelius-White, J. (2007). Learner-centered teacher-student relationships are effective: A meta-analysis. *Review of Educational Research, 77*(1), 113–143. doi:10.3102/003465430298563

Cuéllar, I. (2000). Acculturation and mental health: Ecological transactional relations of adjustment. In I. Cuéllar & F. A. Paniagua (Eds.), *Handbook of multicultural mental health.* New York, NY: Academic Press.

Curby, T. W., Rimm-Kaufman, S. E., & Abry, T. (2013). Do emotional support and classroom organization earlier in the year set the stage for higher quality instruction? *Journal of School Psychology, 51*(5), 557–569. doi:10.1016/j.jsp.2013.06.001.

Curran, M. E. (2003). Linguistic diversity and classroom management. *Theory into practice, 42*(4), 334–340. doi:10.1353/tip.2003.0042.

Daniels, S. & Piechowski, M. M. (2008). Embracing intensity: Overexcitability, sensitivity, and the developmental potential of the gifted. In S. Daniels & M. M. Piechowski (Eds.), *Living with intensity: Understanding the sensitivity, excitability, and emotional development of gifted children, adolescents, and adults.* (pp. 3–17). Scottsdale, AZ: Great Potential Press.

Delpit, L. (2012). "Will it help the sheep?": Why educate? *About Campus, 17*(3), 2–9. doi:10.1002/abc.21080.

Doyle, W. (2006). Ecological approaches in classroom management. In C. Evertson & C. Weinstein (Eds.), *Handbook of classroom management: Research, practice, & contemporary issues* (pp. 97–125). New York, NY: Simon & Schuster Macmillan.

Ducharme, J. M., & Shecter, C. (2011). Bridging the gap between clinical and classroom intervention: Keystone approaches for students with challenging behavior. *School Psychology Review, 40*(2), 257–274.

Duncan G. J., & Magnuson, K. (2011). The nature and impact of early achievement skills, attention skills, and behavior problems. In G. J. Duncan & R. J. Murnane (Eds.), *Whither opportunity? Rising inequality, schools, and children's life chances* (pp. 47–69). New York, NY: Russell Sage and Spencer Foundations.

Duncan, G. J., & Murnane, R. J. (2011). Introduction: The American dream, then and now. In G. J. Duncan & R. J. Murnane (Eds.), *Whither opportunity? Rising inequality, schools, and children's life chances* (pp. 3–25). New York, NY: Russell Sage and Spencer Foundations.

Dunlap, G., Iovannone, R., Wilson, K. J., Kincaid, D. K., & Strain, P. (2010). Prevent-teach-reinforce: A standardized model of school-based behavioral intervention. *Journal of Positive Behavior Interventions, 12*, 9–22. doi: 10.1177/1098300708330880.

DuPaul, G. J., Eckert, T. L., & Vilardo, B. (2012). The effects of school-based interventions for attention deficit hyperactivity disorder: A meta-analysis 1996–2010. *School Psychology Review, 41*(4), 387–412.

Durlak, J. A., Weissberg, R. P., Dymnicki, A. B., Taylor, R. D., & Schellinger, K. B. (2011). The impact of enhancing students' social and emotional learning: a meta-analysis of school-based universal interventions. *Child Development, 82*(1), 405–432. doi:10.1111/j.1467-8624.2010.01564.x.

Dymnicki, A. B., Weissberg, R. P., & Henry, D. B. (2011). Understanding How Programs Work to Prevent Overt Aggressive Behaviors: A Meta-analysis of Mediators of Elementary School–Based Programs. *Journal of School Violence, 10*(4), 315–337. doi:10.1080/153882 20.2011.602599.

Elksnin, L. K., & Elksnin, N. (2004). The social-emotional side of learning disabilities. *Learning Disability Quarterly, 27*(1), 3–8.

Elledge, L. C., Elledge, A. R., Newgent, R. A., & Cavell, T. A. (2015). Social risk and peer victimization in elementary school children: The protective role of teacher-student relationships. *Journal of Abnormal Child Psychology*, 1–13. doi:10.1007/s10802-015-0074-z.

Emmer, E. T. & Sabornie, E. J. (Eds.) (2015). *Handbook of classroom management, 2nd Edition.* New York, NY: Routledge.

Epstein, M., Atkins, M., Cullinan, D., Kutash, K., & Weaver, R. (2008). *Reducing Behavior Problems in the Elementary School Classroom: A Practice Guide* (NCEE #2008-012). Washington, DC: National Center for Education Evaluation and Regional Assistance, Institute of Education Sciences, U.S. Department of Education. Retrieved from http://ies.ed.gov/ncee/wwc/publications/practiceguides.

Erten, O., & Savage, R. S. (2012). Moving forward in inclusive education research. International Journal of Inclusive Education, 16, 2, 221–233. doi: 10.1080/13603111003777496.

Evans, J., Harden, A., & Thomas, J. (2004). What are effective strategies to support pupils with emotional and behavioural difficulties (EBD) in mainstream primary schools? Findings from a systematic review of research. *Journal of Research in Special Educational Needs, 4*, 2–16. doi: 10.1111/J.1471-3802.2004.00015.x

Every Student Succeeds (ESSA) Act of 2015, Pub. L. No. 114-95 (2015).

Farrington, D. P., Ttofi, M. M., & Lösel, F. (2011). Editorial: School bullying and later offending. Criminal Behaviour and Mental Health, 21, 77–79. doi: 10.1002/cbm.807.

Feeney, B. C., & Collins, N. L. (2015). Thriving through relationships. *Current Opinion in Psychology, 1,* 22–28. doi: 10.1016/j.copsyc.2014.11.001.

Fifer, F. L. (1986). Effective classroom management. *Academic Therapy, 21*(4), 401–410. doi: 10.1177/105345128602100402.

Flora, S. R. (2000). Praise's magic reinforcement ratio: Five to one gets the job done. *The Behavior Analyst Today, 1*(4), 64–69. doi:10.1037/h0099898.

Forness, R. S., Kim, J., & Walker, M. H. (2012). Prevalence of students with EBD: Impact on general education. *Beyond Behavior, 21*(2), 3–10.

Forsetlund, L., Chalmers, I., & Bjørndal, A. (2007). When was random allocation first used to generate comparison groups in experiments to assess the effects of social interventions? *Economics of Innovation and New Technology, 16*(5), 371–384.

Fox, L., Carta, J., Strain, P. S., Dunlap, G., & Hemmeter, M. L. (2010). Response to intervention and the pyramid model. *Infants and Young Children, 23*(1), 3–13. doi: 0.1097/IYC.0b013e3181c816e2.

Free, J. L. (2014) The importance of rule fairness: the influence of school bonds on at-risk students in an alternative school, Educational Studies, *40*(2), 144–163, DOI: 10.1080/03055698.2013.858614.

Gagné, F. (2005). From gifts to talents: The DMGT as a developmental model. In R. J. Sternberg & J. E. Davidson (Eds.), *Conceptions of giftedness* (2nd ed., pp. 98–120). Cambridge, UK: Cambridge University Press.

Galindo, C., & Fuller, B. (2010). The social competence of Latino kindergartners and growth in mathematical understanding. *Developmental Psychology, 46*(3), 579–592. doi:10.1037/a0017821.

García Coll, C., & Marks, A. K. (2011). *The immigrant paradox in children and adolescents: Is becoming American a developmental risk.* Washington, DC: American Psychological Association.

Gartstein, M. A., Slobodskaya, H. R., Zylicz, P. O., Gosztyla, D., & Nakagawa, A. (2010). A cross-cultural evaluation of temperament: Japan, USA, Poland and Russia. *International Journal of Psychology and Psychological Therapy, 10*(1), 55–75.

Gay, G. (2010). *Culturally responsive teaching: Theory, research, and practice.* Teachers College Press.

Gehlbach, H., Brinkworth, M. E., & Harris, A. D. (2012). Changes in teacher–student relationships. *British Journal of Educational Psychology, 82*(4), 690–704.

Goh, A. E., & Bambara, L. M. (2012). Individualized positive behavior support in school settings: A meta-analysis. *Remedial and Special Education, 33*(5), 271–286. doi: 10.1177/0741932510383990.

Gone, J. P. (2011). Is psychological science a-cultural? *Cultural Diversity & Ethnic Minority Psychology, 17*, 234–242. doi:10.1037/a0023805.

Gonzales, N., Fabrett, F., & Knight, G. (2009). Acculturation, enculturation, and the psychological adaptation of Latino youth, In F. A. Villarruel, G. Carlo, J. Grau, M. Azmitia, N. Cabrera, & T. Chahin (Eds.), *Handbook of U.S. Latino psychology* (pp. 115–133). Thousand Oaks, CA.: Sage Publications.

Gottman, J. M., & Levinson, R. W. (1992). Marital processes predictive of later dissolution: Behavior, physiology, and health. *Journal of Personality and Social Psychology, 63*(2), 221–233. doi:10.1037/0022-3514.63.2.221.

Gregory, A., Skiba, R. J., & Noguera, P. A. (2010). The achievement gap and the discipline gap: Two sides of the same coin? *Educational Researcher, 39*(1), 59–68. doi:10.3102/0013189X09357621.

Gutman, L. M., & McLoyd, V. C. (2000). Parents' management of their children's education within the home, at school, and in the community: An examination of African-American families living in poverty. *The Urban Review, 32*, 1–24.

Hagenauer, G., Hascher, T., & Volet, S. E. (2015). Teacher emotions in the classroom: Associations with students' engagement, classroom discipline and the interpersonal teacher-student relationship. *European Journal of Psychology of Education, 30*(4), 385–403. doi:10.1007/s10212-015-0250-0.

Halgunseth, L. C., Ispa, J. M. and Rudy, D. (2006), Parental Control in Latino Families: An Integrated Review of the Literature. Child Development, 77: 1282–1297. doi: 10.1111/j.1467-8624.2006.00934.x.

Hébert, T. P., & Kelly, K. R. (2006). Identity and career development in gifted students. In F. A. Dixon & S. M. Moon (Eds.), *The handbook of secondary gifted education* (pp. 35–63). Waco, TX: Prufrock Press.

Hemphill, F. C., & Vanneman, A. (2011). *Achievement gaps: How Hispanic and white students in public schools perform in mathematics and reading on the National Assessment for Educational Progress* (NCES 2011-459). National Center for Education Statistics, Institute of Education Sciences, Washington, DC. Retrieved from http://nces.ed.gov/nationsreportcard/studies/gaps/.

Hibel, J., Farkas, G., & Morgan, P. L. (2010). Who is placed into special education? *Sociology of Education, 83*(4), 312–332. doi: 10.1177/0038040710383518.

Hickey, D., & Schafer, N. J. (2006). Design-based, participation-centered approaches to classroom management. In C. Evertson & C. Weinstein (Eds.), *Handbook of classroom management: Research, practice, & contemporary issues* (pp. 281–308). New York, NY: Simon & Schuster Macmillan.

Hieneman, M., Dunlap, G., & Kincaid, D. (2005). Positive support strategies for students with behavioral disorders in general education settings. *Psychology in Schools, 42*, 779–794. doi: 10.1002/pits.20112.

Hirai, M., Vernon, L. L., Popan, J. R., & Clum, G. A. (2015). Acculturation and enculturation, stigma toward psychological disorders, and treatment preferences in a Mexican American sample: The role of education in reducing stigma. *Journal of Latina/o Psychology, 3*(2), 88–102.

Howard, T. (2010). *Why race and culture matter in school: Closing the achievement gap in America's classrooms.* New York, NY: Teacher's College Press.

Huberman, M., Navo, M., & Parrish, T. (2012). Effective practices in high performing districts serving students in special education. *Journal of Special Education Leadership, 25*(2), 59–71.

Humes, K. R., Jones A. J., & Ramirez, R. R. (2011). Overview of race and Hispanic origin. 2010 Census Briefs. U.S. Department of Commerce. U.S. Census Bureau Report No. C2010BR-02 at www.census.gov/prod/cen2010/briefs/c2010br-02.pdf.

Individuals with Disabilities Education Act [IDEA], 20 U.S.C. § 1400 (2004). Retrieved August 13, 2009 from http://idea.ed.gov/download/statute.html.

Jeynes, W. (2012). A meta-analysis of the efficacy of different types of parental involvement programs for urban students. *Urban Education, 47*(4), 706–742. doi:10.1177/0042085912445643.

Johnson, T., Weed, L. D., & Touger-Decker, R. (2012). School-based interventions for overweight and obesity in minority school children. *The Journal of School Nursing, 28*(2), 116–23. doi: 10.1177/1059840511426147.

Johnston, P. H. (2004). *Choice words: How our language affects children's learning.* Portland, ME: Stenhouse.

Jones, D. J., Zalot, A. A., Foster, S. E., Sterrett, E., & Chester, C. (2007). A review of childrearing in African American single mother families: The relevance of a coparenting framework. *Journal of Child and Family Studies, 16*(5), 671–683. doi:10.1007/s10826-006-9115-0.

Kapalka, G. M. (2005). Avoiding repetitions reduces ADHD children's management problems in the classroom. *Emotional and Behavioural Difficulties, 10*(4), 269–279. doi: 10.1177/1363275205058999.

Kavale, K. A., & Mostert, M. P. (2004). Social skills interventions for individuals with learning disabilities. *Learning Disability Quarterly, 27*(1), 31. doi: 10.2307/1593630.

Kena, G., Musu-Gillette, L., Robinson, J., Wang, X., Rathbun, A., Zhang, J., Wilkinson-Flicker, S., Barmer, A., & Dunlop Velez, E. (2015). *The Condition of Education 2015* (NCES 2015-144). U.S. Department of Education, National Center for Education Statistics. Washington, DC. Retrieved [9/14/2015] from http://nces.ed.gov/pubsearch.

Kern, L., & Clemens, N. H. (2007). Antecedent strategies to promote appropriate classroom behavior. *Psychology in the Schools. Special Issue: The Practitioner's Edition on Promoting Behavioral Competence, 44*, 65–75. doi: 10.1002/pits.20206.

Kitmitto, S. (2011). *Measuring status and change in NAEP inclusion rates of students with disabilities: Results 2007–09* (NCES 2011-457). U.S. Department of Education. Washington, DC: National Center for Education Statistics.

Klassen, R. M., & Chiu, M. M. (2010). Effects on teachers' self-efficacy and job satisfaction: Teacher gender, years of experience, and job stress. *Journal of Educational Psychology, 102*(3), 741–756. doi: 10.1037/a0019237.

Klugman, J., Lee, J. C., & Nelson, S. (2012). School co-ethnicity and Hispanic parental involvement. *Social Science Research, 41*(5), 1320–1337. doi:10.1016/j.ssresearch.2012.05.005.

Kolker, C. (2012). *The immigrant advantage: What we can learn from newcomers to America about health, happiness, and hope.* New York, NY: Free Press.

Kowalski, R. M., Limber, S. P., & Agatston, P. W. (2008). *Cyber bullying.* Malden, MA: Blackwell.

Lagemann, E. C. (2000). *An elusive science: The troubling history of education research.* Chicago, IL: University of Chicago Press.

Lane, K. L., Menzies, H. M., Bruhn, A. L., & Crnobori, M. (2011). *Managing challenging behaviors in schools: Research-based strategies that work.* New York: Guilford Press.

LeClair, C., Doll, B., Osborn, A., & Jones, K. (2009). English language learners' and non-English language learners' perceptions of the classroom environment. *Psychology in the Schools, 46*(6), 568–577. doi: http://dx.doi.org/10.1002/pits.20398.

Levin, H. (2012). More than just test scores. *Prospects, 42,* 269–284. doi: 10.1007/s11125-012-9240-z.

Liefländer, A. K., Fröhlich, G., Bogner, F. X., & Schultz, P. W. (2013). Promoting connectedness with nature through environmental education. *Environmental Education Research, 19*(3), 370–384. doi: 10.1080/13504622.2012.697545.

Martin, N. K., Schafer, N. J., McClowry, S., Emmer, E. T., Brekelmans, M., Mainhard, T., & Wubbels, T. (2016). Expanding the definition of classroom management: Recurring themes and new conceptualizations. *Journal of Classroom Interaction, 51*(1), 36–45.

Masten, A. S., Herbers, J. E., Desjardins, C. D., Cutuli, J. J., McCormick, C. M., Sapienza, J. K., ...Zelazo, P. D. (2012). Executive function skills and school success in young children experiencing homelessness. *Educational Researcher, 41*(9), 375–384. doi:10.3102/0013189X12459883.

McAdoo, H. P., & Younge, S. N. (2009). *Black families.* Thousand Oaks, CA: Sage Publications.

McClowry, S. G. (2014). *Temperament-based elementary classroom management.* Lanham, MD: Rowman & Littlefield.

McCormick, M. P., O'Connor, E. E., Cappella, E., & McClowry, S. G. (2015). Getting a good start in school: Effects of *INSIGHTS* on children with high maintenance temperaments. *Early Childhood Research Quarterly, 30*(A), 128–139. doi:10.1016/j.ecresq.2014.10.006.

McCoy, & Banks, J. (2012) Simply academic? Why children with special educational needs don't like school. *European Journal of Special Needs Education, 27*(1), 81–97, doi: 10.1080/08856257.2011.640487.

McGrady, P. B., & Reynolds, J. R. (2013). Racial Mismatch in the Classroom Beyond Black-white Differences. *Sociology of Education, 86*(1), 3–17.

McKown, C., & Weinstein, R. S. (2008). Teacher expectations, classroom context, and the achievement gap. *Journal of School Psychology, 46*(3), 235–261. doi:10.1016/j.jsp.2007.05.001.

Mercer, S. H., & DeRosier, M. E. (2010). A prospective investigation of teacher preference and children's perceptions of the student/teacher relationship. *Psychology in the Schools.*

Mergler, A. G., & Tangen, D. (2010). Using microteaching to enhance teacher efficacy in pre-service teachers. *Teaching Education, 21*(2), 199–210. doi: 10.1080/10476210902998466.

Merrell, K. W., Gueldner, B. A., Ross, S. W., & Isava, D. M. (2008). How effective are school bullying intervention programs? A meta-analysis of intervention research. *School Psychology Quarterly, 23*(1), 26–42. doi: 10.1037/1045-3830.23.1.2610.1037/1045-3830.23.1.26.

Murnane, R. (2012). Educational Policy Research: Progress, Puzzles, and Challenges. *REMIE - Multidisciplinary Journal Of Educational Research, 2*(3), 234–250. doi:10.4471/remie.2012.13.

Murnane, R. J., & Nelson, R. R. (2007). Improving the performance of the education sector: The valuable, challenging, and limited role of random assignment evaluations. *Economics of Innovation & New Technology, 16*(5), 307–322. doi: 10.1080/10438590600982236.

National Research Council. (2005). *Advancing scientific research in education.* In L. T. Lauress, L. Wise, & T. M. Winters (Eds.) Center for Education, Division of Behavioral and Social Sciences and Education. Washington, DC: The National Academies Press.

Nishina, A., & Bellmore, A. (2010). When might peer aggression, victimization, and conflict have its largest impact? Microcontextual considerations. *Journal of Early Adolescence, 30,* 5–26. doi: 10.1177/0272431609350928.

No Child Left Behind (NCLB) Act of 2001, Pub. L. No. 107-110, § 115, Stat. 1425 (2002).

Novak, A., & Bartelheim, F. (2012). General education students' changing perceptions of students with special needs. *Current Issues in Education, 15*(2), 1–9.

Nowicki, E. A. (2003). A meta-analysis of the social competence of children with learning disabilities compared to classmates of low and average to high achievement. *Learning Disability Quarterly, 26*(3), 171. doi: 10.2307/1593650.

O'Connor, E. E., Cappella, E., McCormick, M. P., & McClowry, S. G. (2014). An examination of the efficacy of *INSIGHTS* in enhancing the academic learning context. *Journal of Educational Psychology, 106*(4), 1156–1169. doi:10.1037/a0036615.

O'Connor, E. E., Collins, B. A., & Supplee, L. (2012). Behavior problems in late childhood: The roles of early maternal attachment and teacher–child relationship trajectories. *Attachment & Human Development, 14*(3), 265–288. doi:10.1080/14616734.2012.672280.

O'Connor, E. E., Dearing, E., & Collins, B. A. (2011). Teacher-child relationship and behavior problem trajectories in elementary school. *American Educational Research Journal, 48*(1), 120–162. doi:10.3102/0002831210365008.

O'Connor, E., & McCartney, K. (2007). Examining teacher-child relationships and achievement as part of an ecological model of development. *American Educational Research Journal, 44*(2), 340–369. doi:10.3102/0002831207302172.

Ogden C. L., Carroll, M. D., Kit, B. K., & Flegal, K. M. (2014). Prevalence of childhood and adult obesity in the United States, 2011–2012. *Journal of the American Medical Association, 311*(8), 806–814. doi:10.1001/jama.2014.732.

Okazaki, S. (2000). Assessing and treating Asian Americans: Recent advances. In I. Cuéllar & F. A. Paniagua (Eds.), *Handbook of multicultural mental health* (pp. 171–193). New York, NY: Academic Press.

Okazaki, S., & Lim, N. E. (2011). Educational outcomes of Asian American children and adolescents. In F. Leong, L. Juang, D.B. Qin, & H.E. Fitzgerald (Eds.) *Asian American and Pacific Islander children and mental health, vol. 1: Development and context* (pp. 143–168). Santa Barbara, CA: ABC-CLIO.

Olweus, D. (1993). *Bullying at school: What we know and what we can do.* Oxford, UK: Blackwell.

Parmer, S. M., Salisbury-Glennon, J., Shannon, D., & Struempler, B. (2009). School gardens: An experiential learning approach for a nutrition education program to increase fruit and vegetable knowledge, preference, and consumption among second-grade students. *Journal of Nutrition Education and Behavior, 41*, 212–217. doi:10.1016/j.jneb.2008.06.002.

Payne, R. (2015). Using rewards and sanctions in the classroom: Pupils' perceptions of their own responses to current behaviour management strategies. *Educational Review, 67*(4), 483–504. doi:10.1080/00131911.2015.1008407.

Pelham, W. E., & Fabiano, G. A. (2008). *Evidence-based psychosocial treatments for attention-deficit/hyperactivity disorder.* Lawrence Erlbaum: Philadelphia, PA.

Pfeiffer, S. I. (2012). School-based practice in action: Serving the gifted: Evidence-based clinical and psychoeducational practice. Florence, KY: Taylor and Francis.

Pianta, R. C. (1999). *Enhancing relationships between children and teachers.* Washington, DC: American Psychological Association. doi:10.1037/10314-000.

Pianta, R. C., & Walsh, D. J. (1996). *High-risk children in schools: Constructing sustaining relationships.* New York: Routledge. doi:10.4324/9781315811444.

Powers, J. D., Bowen, N. K., & Bowen, G. L. (2010). Evidence-based programs in school settings: Barriers and recent advances. *Journal of Evidence-Based Social Work, 7*(4), 313–331.

Rausch, T., Karing, C., Dörfler, T., & Artelt, C. (2015). Personality similarity between teachers and their students influences teacher judgement of student achievement. *Educational Psychology,* 1–16. doi:10.1080/01443410.2014.998629.

Reardon, S. F. (2011). The widening academic achievement gap between the rich and the poor: New evidence and possible explanations. In G. J. Duncan & R. J. Murnane (Eds.), *Whither opportunity? Rising inequality and the uncertain life chances of low-income children* (pp. 91–115). New York, NY: Russell Sage Foundation.

Reed, F. D., McIntyre, L. L., Dusek, J., & Quintero, N. (2011). Preliminary assessment of friendship, problem behavior, and social adjustment in children with disabilities in an inclusive education setting. *Journal of Developmental and Physical Disabilities, 23*(6), 477–489.

Reijntjes, A., Kamphuis, J. H., Prinzie, P., & Telch, M. J. (2010). Peer victimization and internalizing problems in children: A meta-analysis of longitudinal studies. *Child Abuse and Neglect, 34*, 244–252. doi:10.1016/j.chiabu.2009.07.009.

Reis, H. T., Collins, W. A., & Berscheid, E. (2000). The relationship context of human behavior and development. *Psychological Bulletin, 126*(6), 844–872. doi:10.1037//0033-2909.126.6.844

Reis, H. T., Gable, S. L. (2015). Responsiveness, Current Opinion in Psychology, 1, 67–71. doi: 10.1016/j.copsyc.2015.01.001.

Remmers, H. H. (1928). A diagnostic and remedial study of potentially and actually failing students at Purdue University. *Bulletin of Purdue University: Studies in Higher Education*, IX, 28, No. 12.

Reyes, M. R., Brackett, M. A., Rivers, S. E., White, M., & Salovey, P. (2012). Classroom emotional climate, student engagement, and academic achievement. *Journal of Educational Psychology, 104*(3), 700.

Rimm-Kaufman, S. E., Baroody, A. E., Larsen, R. A., Curby, T. W., & Abry, T. (2015). To what extent do teacher–student interaction quality and student gender contribute to fifth graders' engagement in mathematics learning? *Journal of Educational Psychology, 107*(1), 170–185. doi:10.1037/a0037252.

Rivera, H. H., & Waxman, H. C. (2011). Resilient and nonresilient Hispanic English language learners' attitudes toward their classroom learning environment in mathematics. *Journal of Education for Students Placed at Risk, 16*(3), 185–200. doi:10.1080/10824669.2011.585100.

Robinson, N. M. (2012). Parents and the development and education of gifted students. In C. M. Callahan & H. L. Hertberg-Davis, Eds. *Fundamentals of gifted education: Considering multiple perspectives.* (Chapter 24, pp. 236–247). New York: Routledge.

Robles de Meléndez, W., & Beck, V. (2012). *Teaching young children in multicultural classrooms: Issues, concepts, and strategies.* (4th Ed.). Belmont, CA: Wadsworth.

Rogers, C. (1969). *Freedom to learn: A view of what education might become.* Columbus, OH: Charles Merill.

Romero, A. J., Edwards, L. M., Bauman, S., & Ritter, M. K. (2014). Risk Factors for Latina Adolescents' Mental Health and Well-Being. In *Preventing Adolescent Depression and Suicide Among Latinas* (pp. 35–46). Springer International Publishing.

Romi, S., Lewis, R., & Salkovsky, M. (2015). Exclusion as a way of promoting ttudent responsibility: Does the kind of misbehavior Matter? *The Journal of Educational Research, 108*(4), 306–317. doi:10.1080/00220671.2014.886177.

Rothbaum, F., & Rusk, N. (2011). Pathways to emotion regulation: Cultural differences in internalization. In X. Chen & K. H. Rubin (Eds.), *Socioemotional development in cultural context* (pp. 99–127). New York, NY: The Guliford Press.

Rudasill, K. M., & Rimm-Kaufman, S. E. (2009). Teacher–child relationship quality: The roles of child temperament and teacher–child interactions. *Early Childhood Research Quarterly, 24*(2), 107–120. doi:10.1016/j.ecresq.2008.12.003.

Rudasill, K. M., Reio, T. G., Stipanovic, N., & Taylor, J. E. (2010). A longitudinal study of student–teacher relationship quality, difficult temperament, and risky behavior from childhood to early adolescence. *Journal of School Psychology, 48*(5), 389–412. doi:10.1016/j.jsp.2010.05.001.

Sabol, T. J., & Pianta, R. C. (2012). Recent trends in research on teacher–child relationships. *Attachment & Human Development, 14*(3), 213–231. doi:10.1080/14616734.2012.672262.

Sailor, W., Doolittle, J., Bradley, R., & Danielson, L. (2009). Response to intervention and positive behavior support. In W. Sailor, G. Dunlop, G. Sugai, & R. Horner (Eds.), *Handbook of positive behavior support* (pp. 729–753). New York, NY: Springer.

Santisteban, D. A., Muir-Malcolm, J. A., Mitrani, V. B., & Szapocznik, J. (2002). Integrating the study of ethnic culture and family psychology intervention science. In H. Liddle, D. Santisteban, R. Levant, & J. Bray (Eds.), *Family psychology: Science-based interventions* (pp. 331–352). Washington, DC: American Psychological Association Press.

Schaps, E., Battistich, V., & Soloman, D. (2004). Community in school as key to student growth: Findings from the child development project. In J. Zins, R. Weissberg, M. Wang, & H. Walberg (Eds.), *Building academic success on social and emotional learning: What does the research say?* (pp. 189–205). New York, NY: Teachers College Press.

Schleicher, A., & Davidson, M. (2012). *Programme for international student assessment (PISA) results from PISA 2012.* Retrieved from: http://www.oecd.org/unitedstates/PISA-2012-results-US.pdf.

Shapiro, E. S. (2004). *Workbook to accompany academic skills problems: Direct assessment and intervention* (2nd ed.). New York, NY: Guilford.

Sheridan, S. M., Bovaird, J. A., Glover, T. A., Garbacz, S. A., & Witte, A. (2012). A randomized trial examining the effects of conjoint behavioral consultation and the mediating role of the parent-teacher relationship. *School Psychology Review, 41*(1), 23.

Shernoff, D. J., & Csikszentmihalyi, M. (2009). Flow in schools: Cultivating engaged learners and optimal learning environments. In R. Gilman, E. S. Huebner & M. J. Furlong (Eds.), *Handbook of positive psychology in schools* (pp. 131–145). New York, NY: Routledge.

Singh, G. K., & Ghandour, R. M. (2012). Impact of neighborhood social conditions and house-hold socioeconomic status on behavioral problems among US children. *Maternal and Child Health Journal, 16*, 158–69. doi: 10.1007/s10995-012-1005-z.

Sirin, S. R. & Fine, M. (2008). *Muslim American Youth: Understanding hyphenated identities through multiple methods.* New York University Press: New York.

Sirin, S. R., Ryce, P., & Mir, M. (2009). How teachers' values affect their evaluation of children of immigrants: Findings from Islamic and public schools. *Early Childhood Research Quarterly, 24*(4), 463–473. doi:10.1016/j.ecresq.2009.07.003.

Skinner, B. F. (1938). *The behavior of organisms: An experimental analysis.* New York: Appleton-Century.

Slavin, R., & Madden, N. A. (2011). Measures inherent to treatments in program effectiveness reviews. *Journal of Research on Educational Effectiveness, 4*(4), 370–380.

Solomon, A. (2012). *Far from the tree: Parents, children, and the search for identity.* New York: Scribner.

Solomon, D., Watson, M., Battistich, V., Schaps, E., & Delucchi, K. (1996). Creating classrooms that students experience as communities. *American Journal of Community Psychology, 24*, 719–748. doi:10.1007/BF02511032.

Spilt, J. L., Koomen, H. M., Thijs, J. T., & Leij, A. V. (2012). Supporting teachers' relationships with disruptive children: The potential of relationship-focused reflection. *Attachment & Human Development, 14*(3), 305–318. doi:10.1080/14616734.2012.672286.

Stanovich, P. J., & Stanovich, K. E. (2003). *Using research and reason in education: How teachers can use scientifically based research to make curricular & instructional decisions.* National Institute for Literacy. Jessup, MD: Ed Pubs.

Sternberg, R. J. (2012). Intelligence. *Wiley Interdisciplinary Reviews: Cognitive Science, 3*(5), 501–511.

Stoughton, E. H. (2007). "How will I get them to behave?": Pre-service teachers reflect on classroom management. *Teaching and Teacher Education, 23,* 1024–1037. doi: 10.1016/j.tate.2006.05.001.

Suárez-Orozco, C., & Suarez-Orozco, M. M. (2001). Children of immigrants. Cambrideg, MA: Harvard University Press.

Suárez-Orozco, C., Gaytán, F. X., Bang, H. J., Pakes, J., O'Connor, E., & Rhodes, J. (2010). Academic trajectories of newcomer immigrant youth. *Developmental Psychology, 46*(3), 602–618. doi:10.1037/a0018201.

Suárez-Orozco, C., Suárez-Orozco, M. M., & Todorova, I. (2008). *Learning in a new land: Immigrant students in American society.* Cambridge, MA: Harvard University Press.

Südkamp, A., Kaiser, J., & Möller, J. (2012). Accuracy of teachers' judgments of students' academic achievement: A meta-analysis. *Journal of Educational Psychology, 104*(3), 743–762. doi:10.1037/a0027627.

Sugai, G., Sprague, J. R., Horner, R. H., & Walker, H. M. (2000). Preventing school violence: The use of office discipline referrals to assess and monitor school-wide discipline interventions. *Journal of Emotional and Behavioral Disorders. Special Issue: School Safety-Part 1, 8*(2), 94–101. doi: 10.1177/106342660000800205.

Super, C. M., & Harkness, S. (1986). The developmental niche: A conceptualization at the interface of child and culture. *International Journal of Behavioral Development, 9,* 545–569. doi: 10.1177/016502548600900409.

Tamis-LeMonda, C. S., Briggs, R. D., McClowry, S. G., & Snow, D. L. (2008). Challenges to the study of African American parenting: Conceptualization, sampling, research approaches, measurement, and design. *Parenting: Science and Practice, 8*, 319–358. doi:10.1080/15295190802612599.

Tenebaum, H. R., & Ruck, M. D. (2007). Are teachers' expectations different for racial minority than for European American students? a meta-analysis. *Journal of Educational Psychology, 99*(2), 253–273. doi:10.1037/0022-0663.99.2.253.

The New Teacher Project. (2013). *Perspectives of irreplaceable teachers.* Retrieved August 19, 2013, from http://tntp.org/assets/documents/TNTP_Perspectives_2013.pdf.

Tribiano, J. J. U.S. Department of Agriculture, Food and Nutrition Service. (2012). *Agency information collection: Proposed collection; comment request—supplemental nutrition assistance program, administrative review requirements—food retailers and wholesalers* (2012–7033). Retrieved from website: http://www.gpo.gov/fdsys/pkg/FR-2012-03-23/pdf/2012-7036.pdf, 1363-1375.

Trommsdorf, H., & Cole, P. M. (2011). Emotion, self-regulation, and social behavior in cultural contexts. In X. Chen & K. Rubin (Eds.), *Socioemotional development in cultural context.* (pp. 131–163). New York, NY: The Guliford Press.

Ttofi, M. M., & Farrington, D. P. (2011). Effectiveness of school-based programs to reduce bullying: A systematic and meta-analytic review. *Journal of Experimental Criminology, 7,* 27–56. doi:10.1007/s11292-010-9109-1.

U. S. Census Bureau. (2010). An overview: Race and Hispanic origin and the 2010 census. Retrieved from http://www.census.gov/.

U. S. Department of Education, National Center for Education Statistics. (2012). *Digest of Education Statistics, 2011* (NCES 2012-001), Introduction and Chapter 2; U.S. Department of Education, National Center for Education Statistics, Schools and Staffing Survey, Teacher Data Files, 2007–08. Retrieved from http://nces.ed.gov/FastFacts/display.asp?id=28.

U. S. Department of Education. (2007). *Final Guidance on Maintaining, Collecting, and Reporting Racial and Ethnic Data to the U.S. Department of Education.* Federal Register Volume 72, Number 202, Pages 59266-59279. Retrieved from http://www.gpo.gov/fdsys/pkg/FR-2007-10-19/html/E7-20613.htm.

U. S. Department of Health and Human Services (2012). The poverty guidelines. 42 U.S.C. 9902(2). Retrieved from http://aspe.hhs.gov/poverty/12poverty.shtml.

Vannest, K. J., Temple-Harvey, K., & Mason, B. A. (2009). Adequate yearly progress for students with emotional and behavioral disorders through research-based practices. *Preventing School Failure, 53*(2), 73–83. doi: 10.3200/PSFL.53.2.73-84.

Verschueren, K., & Koomen, H. M. (2012). Teacher–child relationships from an attachment perspective. *Attachment & Human Development, 14*(3), 205–211. doi:10.1080/14616734.2012.672260.

Vincent, C. G., Randall, C., Cartledge, G., Tobin, T. J., & Swain-Bradway, J. (2011). Toward a conceptual integration of cultural responsiveness and schoolwide positive behavior support. *Journal of Positive Behavior Interventions, 13*(4), 219–229. doi:10.1177/1098300711399765.

Wallace, T. L., Sung, H. C., & Williams, J. D. (2014). The defining features of teacher talk within autonomy-supportive classroom management. *Teaching and Teacher Education, 42,* 34–46. doi:10.1016/j.tate.2014.04.005.

Wallman, K. K. Federal Interagency Forum on Child and Family Statistics, (2015). *America's children in brief: Key national indicators of well-being.* Retrieved from website: http://www.childstats.gov/americaschildren/index.asp.

Wang, M. C., Haertel, G. D., & Walberg, H. J. (1993). Toward a knowledge-based for school learning. *Review of Educational Research, 63*(3), 249–294. doi: 10.3102/00346543063003249.

Weinstein, C. S. (1977). Modifying student behavior in an open classroom through changes in the physical design. *American Educational Research Journal, 14*(3), 249–262. doi: 10.3102/00028312014003249.

Weinstein, C. S. (1982). Privacy-seeking behavior in an elementary classroom. *Journal of Environmental Psychology, 2*(1), 23–35. doi: 10.1016/S0272-4944(82)80003-0.

Weinstein, C. S. (1998). "I want to be nice, but I have to be mean": Exploring prospective teachers' conceptions of caring and order. *Teaching and Teacher Education, 14*(2), 153–163. doi: 10.1016/S0742-051X(97)00034-6.

Wheldall, K., & Lam, Y. Y. (1987). Rows versus tables: II. The effects of two classroom seating arrangements on classroom disruption rate, on-task behaviour and teacher behaviour in three special school classes. *Educational Psychology, 7*(4), 303–312. doi: 10.1080/0144341870070405.

Wilcox, K. C. (2012). Diversity as strength: How higher-performing schools embrace diversity and thrive. In A. Honigsfeld & A. Cohen (Eds.), *Breaking the mold of education for culturally and linguistically diverse students: Innovative and successful practices for the 21st century* (pp. 47–60). New York, NY: Rowman & Littlefield Education.

Woods, T. A., Kurtz-Costes, B., & Rowley, S. J. (2005). The development of stereotypes about the rich and poor: Age, race, and family income differences in beliefs. *Journal of Youth and Adolescence, 34*(5), 437–445. doi:10.1007/s10964-005-7261-0.

Yeung, W. J. (2012). Explaining the black–white achievement gap: An intergenerational stratification and developmental perspective. In K. R. Harris, S. Graham, and T. Urdan (Eds.) *APA educational psychology handbook, Vol 2: Individual differences and cultural and contextual factors* (pp. 315–336). Washington, DC: American Psychological Association.

Yoshikawa, H., Aber, J. L., & Beardslee, W. R. (2012). The effects of poverty on the mental, emotional, and behavioral health of children and youth: implications for prevention. *American Psychologist, 67*(4), 272.

Zametkin, A. J., Zoon, C. K., Klein, H. W., & Munson, S. (2004). Psychiatric aspects of child and adolescent obesity: a review of the past 10 years. *Journal of the American Academy of Child & Adolescent Psychiatry, 43,* 134–150.

Zee, M., Koomen, H. M., & Veen, I. V. (2013). Student–teacher relationship quality and academic adjustment in upper elementary school: The role of student personality. *Journal of School Psychology, 51*(4), 517–533. doi:10.1016/j.jsp.2013.05.003.

Zeng, G., Boe, E. E., Bulotsky-Shearer, R. J., Garrett, S. D., Slaughter-Defoe, D., Brown, E. D. & Lopez, B. (2013). Integrating U.S. federal efforts to address the multifaceted problems of children: A historical perspective on national education and child mental health policies. *School Mental Health, 5*(3), 119–131. doi: 10.1007/s12310-012-9096-7.

Index

About the Author

Sandee McClowry, PhD, FAAN, is a professor of counseling psychology and teaching & learning at New York University. She is the developer of an evidence-based intervention, *INSIGHTS into Children's Temperament,* and was the principal investigator of the three federal funded clinical trials that tested its efficacy. She is currently the chair of the American Education Research Association's Classroom Management Special Interest Group.